*Death and Dying in Children's
and Young People's Literature*

Death and Dying in Children's and Young People's Literature

A Survey and Bibliography

by

Marian S. Pyles

McFarland & Company, Inc., Publishers
Jefferson, North Carolina, and London

Library of Congress Cataloguing-in-Publication Data

Pyles, Marian S., 1941–
  Death and dying in children's and young people's literature.

  Bibliography: p. 163.
  Includes index.
  1. Children's literature – History and criticism.
  2. Death in literature. 3. Children and death.
  4. Children's literature – History and criticism –
  Bibliography. 5. Death in literature – Bibliography.
  6. Children and death – Bibliography. I. Title.
  PN1009.5.D43P9 1988   809'.89282   87-46386

ISBN 0-89950-335-7 (50# acid-free natural paper)

Printed in the United States of America.

McFarland Box 611 Jefferson NC 28640

*To my mother, Thelma Harris Schultz,
who gave to me her love of literature,
her love of life.*

Acknowledgments

I want to thank Britton Harwood, former chair of the English Department, Miami University, for giving me the opportunity and the impetus to begin this project, and Mark Plageman, Coordinator of the Humanities, Middletown Campus, Miami University, for helping me overcome practical obstacles. I owe a great deal to the staffs of the Middletown, Ohio, Public Library, and the Gardner-Harvey Library of the Middletown Campus for their cooperation in gathering materials from all over the country, particularly Belinda Martindale, whose unflagging efforts and consistent good cheer made my work easier. Kudos also go to Donna Klaaren, Gary Wheeler, and several other colleagues who introduced me to the joys of word processing and patiently led me through its intricacies. And a special thank you goes to my husband, Karl V. Pyles, for his encouragement and for his confidence in me.

Table of Contents

Preface

Given the opportunity in the early seventies to teach a thematic course, I offered "Aging and Death," both common topics in literature. During that decade, the nation was finally addressing the subject of death. Spurred, perhaps, by the publication of Elisabeth Kubler-Ross's *On Death and Dying* in 1969, sociologists undertook in-depth studies; PBS presented several notable documentaries; hospitals began training grief therapists to work with the terminally ill and their families; and individuals were publishing open, poignant accounts of their loss of a loved one. Caught up with the subject, I determined that future courses would skip growing old and concentrate, instead, on dying. Meanwhile, I continued to teach children's literature. I had realized all along how frequently death occurs as a theme in children's books. Thus with the encouragement of colleagues, friends, and family, I undertook this project, a combination of two subjects that continue to be of special interest to me.

Included in this study are folklore, classics of children's literature, and current books, all readily available in public libraries or through interlibrary loans. Overall, the quality of the literature delighted and impressed me. Several books I rejected immediately because of their inferior style or their absurd premises.

A handful of books that mysteriously appear in bibliographies have absolutely nothing to do with the subject of death. A few are appropriate only for the most sophisticated of child readers; I include them to reach as many readers as possible. In some cases, a book falls into more than one category (both a relative and a pet die, for instance); these I grouped arbitrarily into the category most fitting.

One book, Robert Newton Peck's *A Day No Pigs Would Die*, I now routinely include in both children's literature and the

death and dying course. It represents to me the insights and
the joy I have gained in my research. I hope that children, too,
shall find similar comfort and pleasure in the books recommended
here.

Nothing I cared, in the lamb white days, that time would take me
Up to the swallow-thronged loft by the shadow of my hand,
    In the moon that is always rising,
      Nor that riding to sleep
    I should hear him fly with the high fields
And wake to the farm forever fled from the childless land.
Oh as I was young and easy in the mercy of his means,
    Time held me green and dying
Though I sang in my chains like the sea.

                "Fern Hill"
                Dylan Thomas

Introduction

The forces on one side include hand guns, abandoned refrigerators, leukemia, sharks, and nuclear war. The forces on the other include religion, heart transplants, jogging, MADD, and cholesterol-free diets. The first side always wins in the end. We all must die. Yet nearly all adults, particularly in the United States, particularly in the twentieth century, persist in denying this ultimate truth.

Certainly adult language dealing with death affirms this denial: The dead "look asleep"; people "pass away." The funeral business thrives on our fear of death. Forest Lawn, the Los Angeles cemetery infamous for its wretched excesses, offers burial plots with impressive views or entombment with guarantees against air, water, and insects; even piped-in music is available. The "loved one" lies in a "slumber room" until the "service," after which a "coach" transports the "remains" to a "memorial park" to be deposited in a "space" that has been "opened."

> It is the function of the funeral director to be a grief therapist. He has relieved the family of every detail, he has revamped the corpse to look like a living doll, he has arranged for it to 'nap' for a few days, he has put on a well-oiled performance in which the concept of death has played no part what-so-ever. He has done everything in his power to make the funeral a real pleasure for everyone concerned (Mitford 77).

1

Our unfortunate treatment of the old, likewise, is an attempt to cast away tangible evidence of mortality. In past centuries, the aged remained an integral part of the family. Today, we have established retirement communities, "the segregation and isolation of those most likely to die before they actually do so," so that we may "avoid death almost entirely and mute the grief and anguish of bereavement" (Fulton 34).

On a more personal level, otherwise sensible, responsible adults refuse to make out a will, fearing, presumably, that if they sign a legal document dealing with their demise, they are somehow officially decreeing their mortality.

While many simply ignore the inevitability of death, others consciously defy it, assuming that if they can cheat death once, twice, a number of times, they have become immune to it. Thus adults sky-dive, race cars, become war heroes. Such characters abound in literature—Lewis, for instance in James Dickey's *Deliverance*. Almost a caricature of a macho man, Lewis thrives on challenge, seeking out danger so that he may prove himself worthy. Principally, he anticipates a nuclear holocaust from which he will emerge one of the few survivors, totally prepared to live in the wilds.

> "I just believe ... that the whole thing is going to be reduced to the human body, once and for all. I want to be ready.... I think the machines are going to fail, the political systems are going to fail, and a few men are going to take to the hills and start over" (42).

To this end, he continually builds up his body and continually tests himself. He brags of a previous experience when he had to crawl three miles with a broken ankle. A canoe trip down a river in Georgia, around which the novel centers, is to be yet another trial of his abilities and endurance.

The challenges Lewis and his three companions, Ed, Bobby, and Drew, face certainly surpass Lewis's expectations. Traveling in one canoe, Ed and Bobby encounter two hill people. One man rapes Bobby at gunpoint. As the other attempts to rape Ed, Lewis and Drew approach, and Lewis kills one mountain man; the other flees. The four decide not to turn the matter over to legal authorities but instead hastily bury the murdered mountaineer. Now they must face not only the treacherous river but also the other mountain man, who is stalking them. Then Drew is killed, the canoes overturn in rapids, and Lewis is seriously injured. Ironically, it is Ed, not Lewis, who must save them, assuming leadership, scaling a formidable cliff to track down and kill their pursuer, completing the journey down the river, and satisfying the authorities. It is Ed, not Lewis, who must use not only his body but his wits to survive. Because Lewis remains helpless, because his body fails him, he realizes his vulnerability and comes to terms with his own mortality. "He can die now; he knows that dying is better than immortality" (277).

In a lighter vein, Woody Allen's *Death Knocks* presents death as an incompetent klutz, easily bested. In an attempt to make a dramatic entrance, Death climbs up a drainpipe to the second floor of the house of Nat Ackerman, his victim. "'I get my heel caught on some vines, the drainpipe breaks, and I'm hanging by a thread. Then my cape begins to tear'" (1146). He asks for a Fresca, then worries that his cut knee may develop gangrene. Nat, obviously reluctant to die, convinces Death to play gin rummy, giving Nat an extra half-hour for each game he wins. Nat not only earns an extra twenty-four hours of life, but has also won $28.00. Death will return the next night for higher stakes—double or nothing. Meanwhile, Death must spend the rest of the night reading newspapers in a hotel lobby since Nat has cleaned him out.

Instead of trying to outwit death as Lewis or Nat do, the central characters in most of Ernest Hemingway's works reflect a more appropriate response to mortality, one which adults should embrace. Much of Hemingway's work revolves around a central theme, his code: Grace under pressure. He measures his characters by their success in following this code. Adults do not whine about their fate. The ultimate pressure, of course, is death. Hemingway's ultimate heroes, then, are those who face possible death with dignity and with grace. A perfect example is the title character of "The Short Happy Life of Francis Macomber." Born into affluence, pampered and protected, trapped in a marriage of convenience, Macomber has never challenged life—or faced death. At the beginning of the story, on safari, Macomber has just publicly exposed himself as a coward by running in panic from a wounded lion (he has outrageously suggested that the lion be ignored even at the expense of its suffering or the risk of its hurting someone else).

Later, through a series of fortunate coincidences, Macomber fearlessly pursues and wounds a massive buffalo. He feels a "drunken elation," an "unreasonable happiness.... For the first time in his life he really felt wholly without fear" (428). Finally, he declares to Wilson, the safari guide, "'You know, I'd like to try another lion.... I'm really not afraid of them now. After all, what can they do to you?'" (429). Wilson agrees: "'Worst one can do is kill you'" (429). Having embraced the code, Macomber is now ready to face challenge: Once again, he must go into the bush to finish off a wounded animal. When the buffalo charges, Macomber's wife, Margot, grabs a gun, shoots "at the buffalo ... as it seemed to gore Macomber," and hits "her husband about two inches up a little to one side of the base of his skull" (432). Has Margot shot him on purpose because, as Wilson accuses, "'He *would* have left you too'" (433)? Endless debate reveals no clear answer. But the ending is not, as some critics have suggested, cheap trickery. Actually, whether Macomber has died by accident or by intent does not matter. His death simply emphasizes Hemingway's point: Death is always lying in wait. However, Macomber's life is "happy" although "short." In the last few minutes of his time on earth, he has come to terms with his own mortality and is no longer afraid.

Some critics of Hemingway legitimately argue that most of us seldom face the physical challenges he thrived on in his life and in his work — a charging lion, war, the high seas. Nevertheless, our mortality is something we must come to terms with, whatever the agent. And Hemingway's belief that most men die without ever having lived parallels Kubler-Ross's wise philosophy that death is an integral part of life that sets limits, urging us to be productive of our life. Dying takes no skill or understanding. It is living that is difficult.

One of life's difficulties is dealing not with our own death, but with the death of those we love. Our own death may lie in the distant future; the death of a friend or a relative we cannot ignore. How do we cope?

Immediately after the death, a myriad of minor but annoying problems will usually emerge. Embarrassment runs rampant because everyone is uncomfortable. Words of intended comfort are often ludicrous (my sister, for instance, concerned but addled, once blurted out to a girl who had just lost her mother, "Shape up or ship out"). At other times, we are thoughtless — for example, saying to a parent who has just lost a child, "Well, at least you have another child." The bereaved, likewise, don't know what "acceptable" behavior is. Should one cry openly? Should one maintain a stony calm? And certainly, no matter how one behaves, a critic will usually surface: "She didn't shed a tear at the funeral. How heartless!" "Look at him carry on. Doesn't he have any respect?" Shock, fatigue, even family disagreements about funeral arrangements make the first few days after a death debilitating.

These struggles are secondary, however, to the real grief process that must occur if one is to survive the loss and go on to lead a productive life. Once again, literature throughout the centuries has dealt with the varied reactions to loss, from the melancholy of Poe to the celebration of Whitman, from the cynicism of Housman to the revolt of Camus. These observations range from the philosophical to the personal, capturing the many stages psychologists and psychiatrists agree that the bereaved must pass through in order to accept their loss and get on with their lives.

Some people may begin the process before the death occurs because the friend or relative has suffered a long terminal illness; others must begin to adjust after an unexpected death. In any case, the first two stages center around love for the deceased and around loss. The bereaved suffer physiological difficulties. They may have trouble breathing, eating, digesting, and sleeping; they suffer loss of energy and exhaustion. Next, they become preoccupied with thoughts of the deceased, unable to concentrate on anything else. A period of guilt sets in. The bereaved remember slights, omissions, misunderstandings in their relationships with the deceased. Anger follows: anger at the medical staff who failed to keep the person alive; anger at others, both friends and family, who try to give comfort; finally, anger at the person who has died and thus deserted the bereaved. The resulting depression often leads to disorganization, frenzied activity without direction, an inability to function in social situations. Once the bereaved have passed through these stages, they are usually ready to join life again, pouring their energy into a new love object—a job, a spouse or children, a friend. However painful these reactions are, they are necessary, and delays only increase the pain.

If culture shapes language (the Eskimos, for instance, have many different words for snow since it plays such a prominent role in their lives), by the same token, language can change culture. Changing the words we use to define or describe can also lead to a change in attitude: Hence the woman's movement to rid our language of sexism or the emergence of the word "black," replacing the euphemistic "colored," to indicate not only acceptance but pride. In this vein, a recent term for children, "little people," indicates a healthy awareness that while children differ from adults in size, their rights, their needs, their potential for growth are equally important.

A typical syllabus for a course in death and dying might include such topics as war, old age, disease, accidents, disaster, suicide, and murder. What child is exempt from the possibility of or exposure to these occurrences? Some psychologists suggest that even an infant is aware of the process of life and death, being and non-being, loss and return. When his mother leaves, the infant suffers a loss and grieves. Later, as he begins to play, he repeatedly drops a toy and awaits its return by a willing adult. He plays peek-a-boo, disappearing and reappearing; the term even stems from the Old English words meaning "Alive or Dead" (Kastenbaum 95). Nearly all psychologists would agree that by the time a child is three, he is aware that people and things die, although he may deny death as a regular or final process. From ages five to nine, he will accept death, although he will have difficulty accepting his own mortality. Around the age of nine, the child will usually begin to face his own death (Grollman 5–6).

Recognizing this awareness of death, understanding a child's view of death and his reactions to it, and finding appropriate ways of helping him cope with it have three purposes: Adults can help alleviate a child's often unspoken fears; they can help him deal with the loss of a pet, a friend, or a relative; and perhaps the child will grow up, unlike most adults, with a firm perspective on death.

Adults can reason; adults can rationalize; adults can deal with abstractions. If adults have problems dealing with death, children face an even bigger challenge. Because children are unable to understand symbolism and are therefore quite liberal, religious interpretations of death mislead and confuse them (Grollman 11). And explaining that God has taken the person away because He loves that person can lead to disaster: anger at God, or fear that the child himself or someone he loves may die because of God's "love."

Well-meaning adults make other mistakes as well in their attempt to explain death to a child.

Until the age of five, a child thinks of death as impermanent. The deceased has gone away but of course will return. A friend's son, age four, could not understand what had happened to a little girl in his nursery school who had been electrocuted. His mother explained that Angie had died and had been buried in the earth. Later that week, she found him and several of his playmates digging in the backyard, "trying to find Angie so that we can play with her." Saturday morning cartoons may perpetuate this mistaken belief (Kastenbaum 99). How many times is Roadrunner squashed by a boulder or catapulted over a cliff only to return in the next scene, hale and hearty? Thus to tell a child that his mother has "gone on a trip" denies reality initially and later leads to a feeling of abandonment (one of the usual responses of a child to the death of a parent) and then to deep resentment.

Again, well-meaning adults, in an effort to protect the child, may deny him his proper part in the grieving process by keeping him away from the funeral. For a brief period in our history, people questioned the funeral ceremony, labeling it barbaric and insisting that the body not be shown. We now know that the funeral remains a significant rite. It is a means of public announcement of the death, it confirms the reality of the death, it is part of the mourning process, and it affirms family and social solidarity. While no child should be forced to participate, the funeral is normally therapeutic for him as well.

> The presence of a child at a funeral permits the child to recognize that death has occurred. He sees that he is only one among several who is experiencing the loss. Further, depending upon his relationship to the deceased, he may receive comfort, support, and expressions of love and affection from relatives and friends who normally would not be so demonstrative toward him.... Moreover, the child may fear his own involvement in the death. The responses of the others can serve to assure him that he is not culpable (Fulton 47).

Overall, the child must come to realize that "with death, life stops, the deceased cannot return, and the body is buried" (Grollman 8)—but life will go on. Before he comes to this realization, however, he must go through a number of possible stages, similar to those adults go through.

While adults usually feel some remorse at the death of a loved one, children feel actual guilt. Probably every child in a moment of anger has wished a parent dead or expressed hatred of the parent. Then, if the parent dies, the child feels he has been the cause. Or he may feel that because he has misbehaved or failed to obey, the death of a parent is just punishment or that the child will receive additional punishment because of the death. At the same time, he may also be angry, usually at the deceased for abandoning him. Attendant to this anger are both depression and resentment. A child, in more extreme cases, may begin to idealize the dead, refusing to remember anything negative. He may, for a time, even try to assume the mannerisms of the deceased. And he may undergo recurrent panic at the fear of more desertion through death by those he loves. Eventually, however, he will accept—if he is allowed to express his grief and if he can come to terms with the ultimate reality of death. Literature can help.

Literature remains for all of us, children and adults alike, a constant resource. For millions of us, books are a primary avocation, a readily available and totally satisfying diversion. As avid readers, we know, too, literature as a source of escape. Those of us who cannot tolerate sustained suffering can turn to a book—a mystery story, a favorite collection of poetry, a biography—and for a few hours gain some respite. We may also cope more successfully if the book gives us perspective. If we read, for instance, of a character whose suffering far overshadows ours, we will realize that our problems are not really that profound or unmanageable. Or we may find comfort in knowing that we are not alone, that others suffer—and survive.

In other instances, we can grow. Authors frequently point out human foibles and we as readers can feel superior to characters exhibiting foolish attitudes, unproductive behavior; we would never be guilty of such impulses. Sometimes, when authors create genuine pathos and we respond accordingly, we increase our empathy and our compassion for others.

The greatest power of literature, however, is the understanding it offers: understanding of ourselves, our relationships with others, the world around us. We can read extensively in biology, geography, philosophy, psychology, history, sociology, physics, and reli-

gion. All of these aspects of the world are also the material of literature, but in literature we have a dramatization of these forces at
work. The writer gives us his particular vision of the world to ponder, to accept, to reject, to adapt to our own understanding. Robert
Frost defines a poet as someone who tells us something we didn't
know we knew. When we discover these truths, these insights, we
immediately respond, and they follow us the rest of our lives, helping us gain focus and clarification.

Years ago, a student of mine complained that a poem under discussion was "dirty," and thus not acceptable material (she referred
not to the explicit sexual nature of the poem but to its setting of a
junkyard, complete with dust, rust, and bothersome insects). Poetry, she demanded, should deal only with the beautiful. In another
course, an older student complained against assigning Camus's *The
Plague* to young college students because its pessimism would destroy all initiative in them. Both students have a distorted view of
literature. If literature is to mirror life, then all of life is its province.
A.E. Housman, in his poem "Terrence, this is stupid stuff," gives a
superb defense of literature dealing with the more unpleasant truths
of life. Answering his critics' complaint that his poetry is too melancholy, he tells them that if they want to dance, to feel joy, "There's
brisker pipes than poetry" (17). If they want to escape the misery of
life, they must stay drunk. However, since they will surely face
problems, reading his poetry will prepare them "to train for ill and
not for good" (48).

> . . .if the snack is sour,
> It should do good to heart and head
> When your soul is in my soul's stead;
> And I will friend you, if I may,
> In the dark and cloudy day.

Indeed, the major purpose of a literature course in death and dying
is the students' understanding and acceptance of death.

Children's books frequently celebrate the joys and infinite pos-
sibilities of life. They likewise traditionally have happier endings
and produce more resolved conflicts. Yet they, too, must deal also
with the unpleasant elements of life.

Children are often reluctant to express their feelings; they may also be unable to express them since their experiences and their vocabulary are limited. Reading about a character with similar problems or similar reactions helps them to articulate and understand. Much of the success of Judy Blume's works lies in her inclusion of sensitive issues that children find difficult to discuss with parents or peers.

Maurice Sendak's *Where The Wild Things Are* is a brilliant book, illustrating this value of literature for children. Unfortunately, many parents, teachers, and librarians have spoken out against it because it is "unpleasant." The picture-story book tells the story of Max, a child of four or five, who "makes michief of one kind or another" * and is sent to his room without his supper. There he fantasizes a long trip to the land of the wild things, monsters, who make him the leader and join him in a "wild rumpus." But Max grows lonely and returns to his room, where his supper awaits him (his mother has relented, and in the picture, we see even a piece of cake on his dinner tray). Max is not a malleable child; neither is he disturbed; he is simply having one of "those" days, which parents around thw world can recognize. Intrinsic in the book are several valuable insights: We can be angry at those we love without destroying that love (both Max and his mother are angry, yet resolve the anger, he returning home where someone loves him "best of all," she bringing him his dinner); Max has expended his anger through fantasy, a preferable outlet; and having become "King of All Wild Things" in his fantasy, being lauded, not ostracized, for his wild behavior, Max has restored a positive self-concept. Children find this book fascinating and compelling, reading it again and again. They are responding to a familiar experience, to familiar emotions; they come away from it with more understanding of the world and feel better about themselves. Books for children dealing with death serve a smiliar purpose.

A somewhat recent and alarming trend in the field of children's literature is bibliotherapy, therapy through books. In essence, proponents of this movement champion literature as a means for children to resolve all their emotional and psychological problems.

Where possible, page numbers are cited for quoted material. However, because children's books, especially picture books, are often unpaginated, page-number citations could not be given for every quote.

In practice, books with little imagination, inferior writing and illustrations, and heavy doses of didacticism are appearing. Books
written solely for their "message" stridently declare that it is acceptable for mommies to work or for boys to cry. Bibliotherapy has two
main drawbacks (in addition to its adherents' pompous claim that
these books can solve all problems). First of all, didacticism simply
does not work.

> The teach-a-lesson story has never been accepted by children.
> Even in the stark days of Puritan theology when books
> abounded devoted to the holy lives and joyous deaths of
> children, the boys and girls found their own antidote for such
> grim fare in the chapbooks with their folk tales of sturdier char-
> acters and livelier action (Ross 249).

Further, these stories are not literature, but pamphlets that foster
superficial attitudes and unrealistic expectations. All children's
books, whatever the genre, must provide entertainment, must deal
with important problems and handle these problems honestly, and
must, above all, have solid characterization and effective style. In
addition, picture books and picture-story books must have superior
illustrations. Bibliotherapy, in its emphasis on telling, not showing,
sacrifices both art and meaning.

Fortunately, much of children's literature, through folklore, the
classics, and modern works, has an abundance of material that
deals tastefully, truthfully, and artistically with the subject of death.
Parents, teachers, and other caring adults can draw on these works
to help a child deal with an immediate death or to begin to accept
death as an integral part of life.

I. Folklore

There was an old woman had three sons
Jerry and James and John.
Jerry was hung and James was drowned,
John was lost and never was found,
So there was an end of her three sons,
Jerry and James and John.

Nursery rhyme

Letters written in the 1860s, preserved by my family, remain a treasure not only for the sense of heritage they bring but for the insights they provide. One man, a Union soldier, writes to his mother from a St. Louis hospital: "I am wounded in the foot leg and face. I am heartily glad that I am no worse. The hospital is full of poor fellows that are cut to pieces." A woman writes in January 1863 of one son, Thomas, who has been taken prisoner—"that was terable to hear mother is all most crazy about him"—and of another son, Joseph who "took the measles and come home and was at home two weeks and died." She concludes, "He was one lovely boy he was loved by every body he had the best turn of any of the boys he was my favorite but i had to give him up aunt." Another letter in March 1865 mentions typhoid, whooping cough, and smallpox. Life a mere hundred and twenty years ago was certainly harsher. No one would deny the many benefits of living in the twentieth century, especially medical advances that make life more comfortable and secure. Unfortunately, this boon has also, perhaps, been responsible for our shifting attitudes toward the death that Robert Fulton points out.

An increasing number of Americans no longer view death as the result of Divine displeasure or as the price of moral trespass;

12

rather, in our modern, secular society death is coming to be seen as the result of personal negligence or of an unforeseen accident. Death is now a temporal matter that man treats much as he would an avoidable illness or physical stigma. . . . Death, like a noxious disease, has become a taboo subject in American society and as such it is the object of much avoidance, denial, and disguise (31-2).

Thus while our ancestors, in many ways, had far more hardships to endure, they also developed a more realistic outlook on life and on death.

Folklore, including nursery rhymes, ballads, fables, folk tales, myths, and epics, has always been the literature of the common people. They fashioned these stories and poems to explain both nature and human relationships, to amuse themselves, and to express their fears and desires. Naturally, since these stories were fashioned by adults for adults, the tales reflect the violence of their existence. Because children themselves had no literature of their own, they "borrowed" adult literature. And parents in past centuries considered their offspring simply miniature adults, not in need of protection from the more unpleasant aspects of life. Children in the past loved folklore; children today continue to revel in its beauty and its insights.

Indeed, a child's first introduction to literature is most likely nursery rhymes; he hears them, learns to recite them, and finally reads them himself, enjoying as well the marvelous illustrations that accompany the verses. Nursery rhymes help to develop a sense of humor in the child, teach him many basic concepts as in "One, Two, Buckle My Shoe," give him a sense of pride when he has mastered their memorization, and above all, introduce him to the wonder of poetry. They may also expose him to the subject of death.

Violence certainly does exist in nursery rhymes. People choke to death, lose limbs, hurl others down stairs, and commit murder.

Death is frequently natural. For instance, several of the poems revolve around natural enmity between species of animals. In one delightful verse, a cat approaches several mice who are spinning in a barn and asks to be let in so that she may help them. After flattering the mice, Pussy is finally allowed to enter, "And Pussy soon laid them all dead on the floor." In another rhyme, a fox on a cold winter's night craftily steals a goose from a farmer:

> The fox and his wife, without any strife,
> Said they never ate a better goose in all their life;
> They did very well without fork or knife,
> And the little ones picked the bones O!
> Bones O! Bones O!
> They did very well without fork or knife,
> And the little ones picked the bones O!

If animals must eat, so must people. Thus other rhymes deal with hunting wild game or butchering livestock.

> Johnny Armstrong killed a calf,
> Peter Henderson got half,
> Willy Wilkinson got the head
> Ring the bell, the calf is dead.

One man feeds his ram a rick of hay twice a day so that the ram grows to gigantic proportions, "And every leg he had, sir,/ Stood on an acre of land." When the owner finally butchers the ram, he is ". . . up to his knees in blood,/ And the boy that held the pail sir,/ Was carried away in the flood." In a particularly rhythmic poem, a little man, with a gun and bullets made of "lead, lead, lead," shoots a little duck "through the middle of the head, head, head."

Occasionally, death is treated humorously. For instance, a guinea pig, leading a totally normal life, ". . . took a whim and fairly died;/ And as I'm told by men of sense,/ He never has been living since." An even more whimsical view of death concerns a cat fight:

> There once were two cats of Kilkenny,
> Each thought there was one cat too many;
> So they fought and they fit,
> And they scratched and they bit,
> Till, excepting their nails
> And the tips of their tails
> Instead of two cats, there weren't any.

Time and time again, children learn in nursery rhymes of the many perils in the world. Ladybird, Ladybird must "fly away home" since her house has burned and all the children gone, "except one/ And that's little Ann." Humpty Dumpty, after his fall, cannot be put together again. Even the familiar "Rock-A-Bye Baby" has the baby hurtling to the ground, "cradle and all."

The permanence of death and the resulting sorrow appear in longer, more melancholy verses. In "Who Killed Cock Robin," we trace the shooting of Cock Robin, the confession, the funeral preparations, the funeral itself, and the aftermath of grief:

> All the birds in the air
> Fell to sighing and sobbing,
> When they heard the bell toll.

The ending of a particularly philosophical rhyme, "A man of words and not of deeds,/ Is like a garden full of weeds," is brutally factual: "And when your heart begins to bleed,/ You're dead, and dead, and dead indeed." In "My dear, do you know," two little children are kidnapped and left in a wood, "Poor babes in the wood! poor babes in the wood!" They die that night, and the robins sadly bring strawberry leaves to cover them, continuing to this day to sing, "Oh! don't you remember the babes in the wood?"

The best rhyme is probably "Solomon Grundy." In depicting the natural progression of days, it depicts the natural sequence of events in a man's life:

> Solomon Grundy
> Born on a Monday,
> Christened on Tuesday,
> Married on Wednesday,
> Took ill on Thursday,
> Worse on Friday,
> Died on Saturday,
> Buried on Sunday;
> This is the end
> Of Solomon Grundy.

Many children, of course, do not take nursery rhymes seriously—nor should they. Further, children may not always "hear" correctly. (The current soap opera "The Young and the Restless" a child may hear as "The Young and the Rest of Us," or he may hear a line in the Lord's Prayer as "Howard be thy name.") Nevertheless, in their first exposure to literature, children are likewise exposed to the potential violence in the world, to "necessary" killing, and to the inevitability of death.

Children from five to ten graduate to more sophisticated forms of folklore. Ballads, story poems often set to music, thrill children because of their lilting rhythms, their concentrated form, their suspense, and their adventure. Once again, the harshness of life predominates, arising from three principal sources. One source is, of course, nature. The title character of "Sir Patrick Spens" is pressed into service by the king, who desperately needs an experienced sailor. Neither Sir Patrick nor his men wish to make the journey, for the weather is ominous and the omens forbidding. Nevertheless, Sir Patrick, out of necessity, and his men, out of loyalty, brave the treacherous seas. But ". . . lang, lang may their ladies sit, . . . e're they see Sir Patrick Spens/ Come sailing to the land" for:

> Half o'er, half o'er to Aberdour
> It's fifty fadom deep,
> And there lies guid Sir Patrick Spens,
> Wi the Scots lords at his feet.

The wife of Usher's Well also loses her three sons to the sea. Wishing for the wind never to cease or the seas to calm until she can see them again, she wills her sons to return for one night, leaving as dawn approaches (a popular superstition for centuries was that the dead could wander only at night). This ballad emphasizes the permanence of death since the three shall not return again.

Another source of death in the ballads is war or political intrigue. The knight in "The Three Ravens" has been slain in battle. In "The Bonny Earl of Murray," the king has ordered Huntly to arrest the earl; instead, the king's agent has killed the man, and the king is lamenting the loss of "The flower amang them a'."

The most haunting and disturbing ballads are those that portray death resulting from the volatile, often barbarous nature of man. Since Barbara Allen has rejected her lover because of a simple slight on his part, he pines away out of love for her. She, too, then must die.

> "O mother, mother make my bed
> O make it soft and narrow;
> Since my love died for me today,
> I'll die for him tomorrow."

An even more treacherous lover appears in "Lord Randall." Returning from a hunting trip, he complains of being tired and "'fain wald lie down.'" As his mother questions his exhaustion – where has he been? did he eat? what did he eat? – the answers become increasingly ominous. He has been to his lover's; he has eaten there; he shared his broth with his bloodhounds. When his mother hears that the dogs have bloated and died, she realizes that Lord Randall has been poisoned. He, of course, has already discovered his lover's betrayal and wishes to lie down not only because he is dying but because he is "'sick at the heart.'"

The most gruesome of all, perhaps, is "Edward." When Edward's mother sees his sword dripping with blood, she asks him what he has killed. After he tries to deceive her by saying that he has killed his hawk, then his horse, he finally reveals the horrible truth: "'O I ha'e killed my fader dear.'" He is fleeing the land, leaving behind him his wife and children to beg for their sustenance. Not until the last stanza does the reader realize that Edward's mother had instigated the horrible deed: "'The curse of hell frae me sal ye bear,/ Sic counseils ye gave to me, O.'"

The most interesting aspect of the tragic ballads is the frequent lack of retribution. The innocent suffer, the guilty go unpunished, and sadness reigns.

While another form of folklore, the fable, deals primarily with precepts for living, it does deal with death in a limited way. The fable is appealing in its brevity and its focus on action. The characters, usually animals, are totally human in their actions and their responses. And the morals, while didactic, still are generally valid (some modern collections omit the moral altogether, allowing the child to figure out the point of the tale; others put the moral on the following page so that the child can test the correctness of his interpretation). Aesop's fables are the most familiar because they are the most comprehensible; other bodies of fables, like the Jatakas from India, are frequently too long or too complex for the child reader, and those of the French fabulist La Fontaine often suffer from fractured translations.

In Aesop's fables, as in nursery rhymes, the natural enmity between species of animals once again emerges: the fox and the hen; the cat and the mouse; the hawk and the pigeon; the hare and the hound. Likewise, animals are frequently the prey of hunters and

fishermen. In other fables, death is often the penalty for stupid behavior. Still others suggest that the world is a dangerous place. Two
fables actually face the subject of death head on. A man, "stooped
by age and hard work," throws his bundle of sticks on the ground
and cries, "'Life is too hard. I cannot bear it any longer. If only
Death would come and take me!'" However, when his wish is an-
swered, when Death appears and asks what he may do for the man,
the latter replies, "'Please, sir, . . . could you please help me put this
bundle of sticks back on my shoulder again?'" (180). While the moral
of the story is, "How sorry we would be if many of our wishes were
granted," the reader will likely see also that no matter how horrible
life seems, it is indeed preferable to death. Similarly, in another
fable, hares who believe themselves "the most persecuted of all the
animals" determine to kill themselves. However, when they approach a lake where they may drown themselves, they frighten a
school of frogs, who all dive into the water; the hares then realize
that "there is always someone worse off than yourself" (79), stressing
once more that life is a struggle, but one worth pursuing.

For pure richness, nothing can match folk tales. Polished
through retelling, they are truly masterpieces of literature. Their re-
fined aspects of style—the brilliant imagery, the rollicking humor,
the vivid poetic refrains, the terse dialogue—all make them highly
readable. Their tight structure—a brief but comprehensive introduction of time, place, characters and conflict, repetition with variety to move the plot, and a swift, predictable ending—provides
both suspense and familiarity. True, the characters are often one-
dimensional, but they do reflect common, often universal personalities. As Arbuthnot and Sutherland point out, Cinderella is a typical teenage girl who dreams of beautiful clothes and has romantic
visions of a handsome young man who will be part of her future
(159). And the themes, the insights into human behavior remain
valid. In folk tales, the child identifies with the poor and the down-
trodden who are nevertheless bright and virtuous. He thrills at the
confrontations with wild animals and with the supernatural—trolls,
giants, and ogres. And he finds comfort in seeing the good triumph,
the evil punished. Folk tales take the child to faraway places, provide him with spine-chilling adventure, and leave him satisfied and
secure.

This security, surprisingly, stems to a great extent from the many insights into death that pervade folk tales. Many possible explanations of the origins of folk tales exist, all valid to some extent. Are they allegories, attempting to explain natural phenomena? Do they have their basis in ancient religions? Do they represent emotional fantasy, nightmares, or wish fulfillment? Whatever their origin, all would seem to depend to some degree on symbolism, and thus a paradox emerges: If children until the age of ten or eleven cannot deal with abstract thought, how then is a child of six or seven able to comprehend these symbolic messages? Bettelheim assures us that the child understands intuitively, "though he does not 'know' explicitly" (179). And we must remember the child's ready acceptance of fantasy. Thus, as Hella Moller suggests, "Stories of death and abandonment serve the function of learning, on the fantasy level, to cope with one's fears and at the same time to reassure oneself of the unreality of these fantasized terrors" (148). In this regard, folk tales may very well provide catharsis to a child. Just as adults view classical tragedies to cleanse themselves of fear or on a more mundane level, flock to current films dealing with the supernatural, with natural disasters, and with murder and mayhem, (frequently at the hands of a mad man), so may children expend their fears through folk tales. Likewise, in answering the charge that folk tales mislead children in the common ending, "And they lived happily ever after," Bettelheim insists that such an ending "does not for a moment fool the child that eternal life is possible" (10). Interestingly enough, other endings do exist that suggest a more realistic view: "They lived happily till they died"; "So he took her back to the royal castle, she was again his dear wife, from whom nothing but death could divide him"; "Then the children went home together as happy as possible, and if they are not dead yet, then they are still alive."

Still another symbolic level that adults find difficult to accept but children are comfortable with is the amazing resurrections. In this case,

> Death is rather a symbol that this person is wished away—just as the oedipal child does not really wish to see his parent-competitor die, but simply wants him removed from the child's way of winning his other parent's complete attention. The child's expectation is that, much as he has wished a parent out of the way

at one moment, the parent should be very much alive and at the child's service in the next (Bettelheim 106).

In "The Raven," we find that not only children are guilty of this fantasy. A queen whose infant daughter has been particularly naughty and difficult to handle wishes, in a moment of pique, her child turned into a raven.

Another symbolic explanation of resurrections is the theme of redemption. In simple terms, a character who has been "killed" because of a foolish mistake comes back to life to be given another chance. Bettelheim says of "Little Red Cap" (more familiarly, "Little Red Riding Hood"):

> The child also understands that Little Red Cap really "died" as the girl who permitted herself to be tempted by the wolf; and that when the story says, "the little girl sprang out" of the wolf's belly, she came to life a different person. This device is necessary because, while the child can readily understand one thing being replaced by another ... he cannot yet comprehend inner transformations. So among the great merits of fairy tales is that through hearing them, the child comes to believe that such transformations are possible (179).

Similarly, in "The Wolf and the Seven Goats," the mother goat, leaving to fetch food, warns her young about the wolf, whom they can recognize by his black paws and his rough voice. They turn the wolf away twice, but the third time, because he has whitened his paws with flour and made his voice soft with chalk, they allow him in, whereupon he swallows all but one. When the mother returns and hears what has happened, she and her remaining kid find the wolf, cut open his belly, release the others, and replace them with stones in the wolf's belly. When he awakens and goes for a drink, the additional weight makes him lose his balance and fall into a well to drown. The goats have been given another chance; from now on they will listen more carefully to their mother's warnings and not be deceived by appearances.

Snow White, too, is given a second chance. Although warned by her friends the dwarfs not to let anyone in, three times does she trust her wicked stepmother in disguise, a woman whose treachery and hostility she certainly fears. After Snow White has eaten the poisoned apple, she is restored when her glass coffin is jiggled and the poisoned bite falls from her mouth.

In a somewhat different vein is the title character of "Faithful John." Having promised his dying king that he will be faithful to the King's son, Faithful John sacrifices himself again and again. The new king, however, misinterprets one of Faithful John's actions to keep the king and his bride safe and has John thrown into jail, where he turns to stone as punishment for his earlier attempts to protect his lord. Only after years have passed does the statue of John speak to the repentant king: "'You can bring me back if you will destroy your best-beloved'" (Jacobi 137). The king must cut off the heads of his two children and smear their blood on John's statue. John is restored to life, and he, in turn, restores the lives of the children. Here, it is the king who is given another chance, who learns the value of trust in those who care for us.

A final symbolic interpretation of folk tales concerns the child's relationship to his parents. If a child tries to leave the security and protection of his parents too early, death will likely result.

> Death of the unsuccessful—such as those who tried to get to Sleeping Beauty before the time was ripe, and perished in the thorns—symbolizes that this person was not mature enough to master the demanding task which he foolishly (prematurely) undertook (Bettelheim 180-1).

For instance, in "The Singing Bone," two sons set off to kill a wild boar in order to collect their king's reward. The younger son, innocent and simple, meets a gnome that gives him a magic spear, enabling the boy successfully to kill the boar. The older son, however, clever and crafty, kills his younger brother and throws him in the river so that he may take credit for ridding the kingdom of menace. Years later, a herdsman finds a little bone and takes it home to use as a mouthpiece for his horn. The bone sings out the tale to the herdsman, who reveals the evil event to the king. After the king discovers the skeleton of the younger son, the older one is drowned, and the bones of the younger son are buried in a beautiful grave. Obviously, the boy was too young and innocent to take on the perils of the world.

In a strange little tale, a mouse, a bird, and a sausage live together, sharing the work and living in harmony. When the bird, however, insists they change chores, all perish: when the sausage attempts to bring back wood from the forest, a dog gobbles it down; when the mouse attempts to get into the pot to stir and flavor the broth as the sausage did, he, of course, dies; and when the bird attempts to fetch water, he falls in and drowns. Obviously, all were attempting tasks for which they were not yet prepared.

Sometimes, the death of an unprepared protagonist occurs not because of a premature attempt on his part, but because of cruel circumstances. In "The Poor Boy in the Grave," a shepherd boy, who has been orphaned, is adopted by rich parents. Because they are greedy, however, they give him little to eat, and they assign to him impossible chores, beating him when he fails. The poor lad actually kills himself. The parents do suffer, living out the rest of their lives in poverty and misery, but their repentance does not really compensate for the fate of the poor child. And only the truly hard-hearted could remain unmoved by the plight of Hans Christian Andersen's "The Little Match Girl." Having lost her slippers, huddled against the cold, fearful of beatings from her father since she has sold not one match, she begins to light the matches, one by one, momentarily having visions of a roast goose, a brilliant Christmas tree, a glowing stove. Lighting the rest of a bundle of matches all at once, she sees her dead grandmother, the only person ever to have loved the little girl, and is transported to God.

Other tales, however, suggest that when one is ready to meet the world, he must not tarry.

> If we try to escape separation anxiety and death anxiety by desperately keeping our grasp on our parents, we will only be cruelly forced out, like Hansel and Gretel. . . . The fairy tale is future-oriented and guides the child . . . to relinquish his infantile dependence on wishes and achieve a more satisfying independent existence (Bettelheim 10–11).

Thus frequently in folk tales, parents determine that their offspring must leave the family home. Clever Elsie's parents determine that "'Our daughter is now grown up and we must get her married soon'" (Jacobi 172). The father in "The Three Children of Fortune," realizing that he is about to die, wants to provide for his three sons. Since he has no money, he gives to them, respectively, a cock, a scythe, and a cat, and advises, "' It rests with yourselves alone to turn my gifts to good account'" (Jacobi 23).

Thus death appears frequently. It may be the result of foolish or nasty behavior, or it may be the means of redemption. In other instances, it is the natural outcome of a long life. In addition to parents and grandparents who must face death because of their age, in two different tales, a dog and a horse face execution because they have outlived their usefulness. Certainly, however, the death of a parent "creates the most agonizing problems, as it (or the fear of it) does in real life" (Bettelheim 9).

Facing the death of a friend or a parent is only one of the struggles. The major insight about death in folk tales is, therefore, that only through struggle does one give meaning to life.

> . . . a struggle against severe difficulties in life is unavoidable, is an intrinsic part of human existence—but that if one does not shy away, but steadfastly meets unexpected and often unjust hardships, one masters all obstacles and at the end emerges victorious. . . . Safe stories mention neither death nor aging, the limits to our existence, nor the wish for eternal life. The fairy tale, by contrast, confronts the child squarely with the basic human predicaments (Bettelheim 8).

Auden mirrors this sentiment: "There is no joy or success without risk or suffering, and those who try to avoid suffering fail to obtain the joy, but get the suffering anyway" (Aesop xvii). Arbuthnot and Sutherland agree:

> . . . that courage and simple goodness work their own magic in this world, that evil must be conquered even if it carries us to the gates of death, and that grace and strength are bestowed upon those who strive mightily and keep honest, kindly hearts (151).

Tom Thumb, that engaging little fellow who braves the world gallantly in spite of his size, realizes that "'This world is full of trouble and sorrow'" (Jacobi 110). Another perfectly delightful protagonist who meets life head-on is the Gallant Tailor. Having killed seven flies at once, he brags to the world that he has killed "Seven at one blow." Everyone, of course, assumes that he is talking about men, not flies, and thus constantly puts him to the test. Throughout, he uses not brute strength but his wits. For instance, when he is given the task of killing two giants in order to win a princess in marriage and half the kingdom, he simply sets them against each other. Another tale, "The Unwelcome Visitors," suggests that even seemingly harmless objects in the world can lead to misery and even death. A cock, a hen, a cat, a millstone, an egg, a duck, a darning needle, and a pin set out to visit Dr. Korbes. There, they lead him on a merry chase. For example, when he plops in his chair, the darning needle stabs him. When he falls into bed, the pin attacks him. Finally, as he tries to run away, down falls the millstone on his head and kills him. "This Dr. Korbes must really have been a very wicked or a very injured man" (Jacobi 175).

Unlike the relatively jolly Tom Thumb and the Gallant Tailor, most characters in folk tales go through debilitating, heartrending experiences. The best example, perhaps, is Andersen's "The Steadfast Soldier." Having only one leg because he was the last of the soldiers to be cast, he suffers a fall from a third-story window. Put into a paper boat, he reaches a canal and is drowned, only to be swallowed by a fish and later cut out of its stomach. Finally, he is thrown into a fire, where he melts in the shape of a heart. His virtue? He has remained steadfast throughout.

The tin soldier's life, however, does have additional merit, for he has lost his heart to the paper maiden, dancing in the paper castle. She, too, has been blown into the fire, and they perish together. The most important insight into death that the folk tales offer is simply that "human beings are always in search of love. There will never be a time when people do not need loving reinforcement against the hostile world and the frightening thought of death" (Arbuthnot and Sutherland 159).

One of the most poignant tales revealing the healing power of love is "Rapunzel." When a pregnant woman craves rampion from the garden of a neighboring witch, her husband steals it for her, only to be caught by the old crone. To insure his safety, he agrees to turn over his child at birth. In due course, he fulfills his part of the bargain. The child, whom the witch names Rapunzel, is kept in a high tower without doors or ladders. Rapunzel lets down her golden hair so that the witch may climb into the tower. One day, a prince hears Rapunzel singing and is entranced. Spying, he sees the witch's ascent to the tower room and deceives Rapunzel into letting him in. They, of course, fall in love, but sadly, Rapunzel lets slip that she has had a visitor. The witch cuts off Rapunzel's hair, sends her into the wilderness, and then traps the prince by letting down the cut tresses of his love. As he falls from the tower, he is blinded by the thorns. For years and years he wanders about, weeping for his lost love. One day, he comes upon his beloved Rapunzel. His sight is restored, and they spend their remaining lives in happiness.

> The folk tale does indicate that which alone can take the sting out of the narrow limits of our time on this earth, forming a truly satisfying bond to another. The tales teach that when one has done this, one has reached the ultimate in emotional security of existence and permanence of relation available to man; and this alone can dissipate the fear of death. If one has found true adult love, the fairy story also tells, one doesn't need to wish for eternal life (Bettelheim 10–11).

Eternal life is available occasionally in the myths, but usually by the time a child is ten or so and ready to delve into this relatively sophisticated form of folklore, he certainly will not interpret these tales literally, but will accept them as a magical blend of fantasy and reality, an imaginative rendering of life and its forces. The child will thrill to early man's attempts to explain the creation of earth and mankind, natural phenomena, and the origins of civilization. Mythology also traditionally explains the forces of evil to help alleviate mankind's fears.

While many cultures have a body of myths, the two deserving the most attention are the Greek myths, later adopted by the Romans, and the Norse myths. Some differences do exist. The harsh climate of Scandinavia probably accounts for the general nature of the Norse myths—an emphasis on war, constant vigilance against evil, and fierce gods who prevail more from strength than from their wits, in contrast to the more leisurely pace, the frequent humor, and the richness of detail in the Greek and Roman myths. Strangely, however, the Norse gods are far kinder to mankind, not interfering in their lives, and frowning upon such practices as human sacrifice, whereas the Greek gods and goddesses are constantly meddling in human affairs and frequently mistreating and abusing mortals. A final difference is that while the Greek gods are immortal, the Norse gods, the Aesir, know that their time on earth is limited: "They too must die . . . like everybody and everything else" (D'Aulaire, *Norse Gods* 30).

Although the principal characters of the myths are gods and goddesses, their all-too-human natures make them believable. In the D'Aulaires' otherwise magnificent *Book of Greek Myths*, their statement that "The Greek gods looked much like people and acted like them, too, only they were taller, handsomer and could do no wrong" (9), is indeed misleading, for the gods frequently exhibit cruel and nasty natures. Hera, for instance, the queen of the Greek gods, because of her jealous nature, repeatedly brings woe to her fellow gods and to human beings alike. And the god Loki in Norse mythology is constantly causing upheaval because of his pride and greed. Out of these petulant personalities and out of the many supernatural monsters preying on earth come high adventure and high drama, guaranteed to keep the reader interested. And the child well-versed in mythology will have a much deeper understanding of the art of Western civilization since so much of our painting, our literature, and our music derives from this rich source.

The ancients' concepts of an afterlife are interesting. The Greeks imagined an underworld, ruled by Hades, where mortals "whirled about forever like dry leaves in a cold autumn wind" (D'Aulaire, *Greek Myths* 56). In Norse mythology, Hel rules over this province; "She did nothing to make her guests happy in her vast hall" (D'Aulaire, *Norse Gods* 50). Some of the dead fare better than others. Greek heroes go to the Elysian Fields, "where they lived happily forever in never-failing light" (D'Aulaire, *Greek Myths* 60). In the Norse myths, dead heroes go to Odin's guest house, Valhalla, for a life of "riotous feasting and fighting" (D'Aulaire, *Norse Gods* 73). In both underworlds, also, are punishments for the wicked. In Hel is a special place, Nifheim, a particularly grim locale, and in Hades, Rhandamanthus, a judge, doles out punishment to the souls of sinners whom the avenging Erinyes whip.

These concepts of an afterlife show that in the myths, as well, mortality is an inevitable part of life. First of all, as Arbuthnot and Sutherland point out, myths "make more acceptable the painful realities of existence—danger, disease, misfortune, death—by explaining them as part of a sacred order in the universe" (190). While this order lies in the hands of gods and goddesses who are sometimes less than admirable, their actions and the results do parallel the forces in this world that lead to pain, upheaval, and death. Further, the events brought about by the gods often serve to test heroes. Thus, as in folk tales, the protagonists strive against evil in order to give life meaning. Similarly, death is frequently a punishment for sins, indicating that because life is indeed short, one must live it honorably: Ixion is "condemned to whirl about forever in the underworld, tied to a flaming wheel" because he has attempted to carry off Hera; Tantalus "stood in water up to his neck, but could never quench his thirst, for whenever he bent to drink, the water receded" (D'Aulaire, *Greek Myths* 96, 112). Because he has sacrificed his own son as a dish for the gods; Sisyphus must push a boulder up a steep hill, only for it to roll again to the bottom, because of the many tricks he has played on Hades.

The ancients wove into their interpretation of the world an explanation of death. Three lesser Greek goddesses are the three Fates who decide how long a mortal will live. "When a mortal was born, Clotho spun the thread of life, Lachesis measured a certain length, and Atropos cut the thread at the end of his life" (D'Aulaire, *Greek Myths* 70). (Similarly, in Norse mythology, the three Fays of Destiny, the Norns, "willed a life of luck or a life of misery, a short life or a long one, for the Norns spun a thread of life for every human being" [D'Aulaire, *Norse Gods* 30].) Because Asclepius, the most renowned Greek physician, is so successful, the Fates complain that their work is in vain, and Hades complains that he is not receiving dead souls. As a result, Zeus destroys Asclepius, and once again, the normal process of life and death continues.

Two myths poignantly emphasize that death is permanent. When the Norse God of Light dies, murdered by his brother through the machinations of the evil Loki, all the gods and all of nature weep, for Balder is the most beloved of the Aesir. Odin's son Hermod travels to the underworld to beg Hel for Balder's release from death. Hel agrees on one condition: Everything in the world must weep for Balder. "Every creature and everything wept—men and women, beasts, birds, trees, flowers, stones, metals—everything living and lifeless shed tears for Balder" (136)—except an old crone (actually Loki in disguise). Thus Balder must remain "in the dark realm of Hell" (136). In a parallel myth of the Greeks, Orpheus, a renowned musician, falls in love with the lovely Eurydice. On their wedding day, however, she is bitten by a serpent and is sent straightway to Hades. Orpheus dares, as no mortal ever has, to travel to the underworld in hopes of releasing Eurydice. Because of his great skill upon the lyre, all the guardians of the underworld are moved and let him enter. Because of his great love for his bride, Orpheus even moves the stern Hades, who agrees to release Eurydice on one condition: As she follows Orpheus out of hell, he must not look back. Full of doubt, since he cannot see or hear his beloved, he looks back just before he reaches the upper world. He sees her for just an instant, she whispers farewell, and then she is gone. Most readers are frustrated by the ending of this myth, denying the major insight: The dead cannot return.

Neatly summing up the major focus of the epics, the last genre of folklore to be considered, is one of Odin's messages to mortals: "'Men die, cattle die, you yourself must die one day. There is only one thing that will not die—the name, good or bad, that you have made for yourself'" (2). The epic heroes are men, not gods. Imbued with almost superhuman characteristics, they nevertheless must die. But they die in pursuit of good. The three most appealing epics are *The Iliad*, the story of the Trojan War, focusing on a number of heroes, principally Achilles, the famous Greek warrior; *The Odyssey*, the story of Odysseus (more commonly known as Ulysses) and his ten-year struggle to reach his home of Ithaca after the Trojan War; and *Beowulf*, the story of a daring Geat who helps rid the Danes of the monster Grendel and its dam and later rids his own kingdom of a menacing dragon. The two most appealing legends (epics based on the lives of people we know actually existed) are King Arthur, who valiantly provides leadership to bring peace to England, and Robin Hood, the outlaw who fights for justice and freedom.

The episodic nature of the epic pits these heroes repeatedly against mortal enemies, against hostile gods and goddesses, against fierce monsters and against nature. The reader trembles as Hector and Achilles meet in battle, as Ulysses and his men encounter a one-eyed giant who devours several of Ulysses's men, as King Arthur and his knights battle other ambitious knights seeking to overthrow the orderly kingdom, as Robin Hood must outwit the wicked Sheriff of Nottingham and his henchmen.

Most of these encounters are incredibly violent.

> Grendel tore his victim limb from limb, picking off arms and
> legs, lapping up the blood with a greedy tongue, taking bites to
> crunch up bones and swallow gory mouthfuls of flesh. In a
> minute, all that was left of the man was a frayed mass of veins
> and entrails hanging from the monster's mouth (45).

Is such violence appropriate for children? Some will revel in it,
particularly boys around eleven or twelve. Most children, of course,
will find these passages repulsive – as they should. Writers who
make violence palatable also make it acceptable. In addition, these
trials emphasize the harshness of life and stress the major insight
into life and death offered by the epics:

> There is nobility of great heroism, of keeping your word even
> though it costs you your life, of self-sacrifice for a great cause, of
> death rather than dishonor, of ideals of race and family, of in-
> trepid courage and perseverance (Arbuthnot and Sutherland
> 202).

These heroes never give up until they meet their fate as mortals and
die. Thetis, mother to Achilles, says to him:

> "My son, there are two lots of life before you, and you may
> choose which you will. If you stay in this land and fight against
> Troy, then you must never go back to your own land, but will
> die in your youth. Only your name will live forever; but if you
> will leave this land and go back to your home, then shall you
> live long, even to old age, but your name will be forgotten"
> (Church 67).

Thus the heroes, in their struggles, fight for those principles
that continue to give life meaning. The knights of the round table
frequently fight dire battles to protect their ladies. Ulysses's constant goal is to reach his home and family. His wife, his son, and
his aging father, in turn, remain faithful to him and weep at the
thought that he might be dead. In *The Iliad*, Priam, the Trojan king,
braves the camp of the Greeks in order to recover the body of his
beloved son, Hector: "'And if I die, what do I care? Let Achilles slay
me if only I may hold the body of my son once more in my arms'"
(133). Friendship, too, is equally important. When Achilles finds
that he has sent his friend Petroclus to his death, he wishes to die.

And Little John, believing Robin Hood dead, declares, "'Now I die joyfully, nor do I care how I die, for life is nought to me!'" (Church 225). Further, when Glaucus, fighting for the Trojans, and the Greek Diomed meet and learn that their fathers were fast friends, they refuse to fight each other. Robin Hood and his men are totally loyal to one another, risking their lives if need be. We see this same loyalty in Beowulf's men.

In spite of the violence in epics, the men are not basically blood-thirsty. Twice the Greeks and the Trojans agree to let two men alone fight to decide the outcome of the war; it is the gods who will not allow this more civilized resolution of the conflict. Robin Hood kills only twice. The first murder would be considered self-defense today. After he has won a wager in an archery contest, his opponent not only refuses to pay the debt but fires an arrow at Robin Hood, who, understandably, shoots back. It is this incident that has made him an outlaw. He repents this deed the rest of his life:

> "But fain would I shun blood and battle, and fain would I not deal sorrow to women folk and wives because good stout yeomen lost their lives. Once I slew a man, and never do I wish to slay a man again, for it is bitter for the soul to think thereon" (Pyle 31).

Near the end of the story, Robin Hood must kill a vicious outlaw whom the Sheriff of Nottingham has commissioned to destroy Robin Hood.

Likewise, while these heroes must exhibit physical courage, they use their wits as well, frequently to avoid actual battle. Ulysses tricks the Cyclops by getting him drunk on wine and by giving as his name "No Man," so that the Cyclops cannot retaliate. Beowulf bests Grendel by strength of will as much as strength of body. And Robin Hood throughout merrily uses disguises and devises ploys to deceive his pursuers.

Indeed, Robin Hood, above all the other epic heroes, gives us the best perspective on life and death. He sees daily the corruption of the state and the church. As an outlaw, he faces possible capture at every moment and must outwit cunning, frequently inhumane foes. And he knows life is short, "' . . . for man is but dust, and he hath but a span to live here till the worm getteth him.'" (Pyle 43). Therefore, he declares, "' . . . so let life be merry while it lasts, say

I'" (43). And merry he is. Even when he plans to rob someone, he and his men give the victim an elaborate feast and entertain him with sports and games. The entire legend is full of exuberance and humor. When Robin Hood dies, we are sorry, of course, but we feel content because he has left a legacy of decency and joy.

As children read of Humpty Dumpty, Little Red Riding Hood, Sir Patrick Spens, Orpheus, and King Arthur, they begin to realize that death is a natural part of life: people kill animals to protect themselves and to provide food; animals kill other animals; both animals and people grow old and die. They also begin to realize just how dangerous a place the world is. Finally, they will begin to realize that mortality only makes life sweeter. Struggle, adherence to principles, and love make the difference.

II. The Death of a Pet

Johnny Armstrong killed a calf.
Peter Henderson got half.
Willy Wilkinson got the head.
Ring the bell, the calf is dead.

Nursery rhyme

The first exposure a child has to death is likely to be the loss of a pet. Obviously, not all children will react alike. On a classic episode of "The Bill Cosby Show," five-year-old Rudy loses her pet goldfish. Anticipating her grief, Dr. Huxtable coerces the entire family into participating in a funeral, with formality and proper dress (he will not even allow his wife to wear earrings). However, as they all gather around the toilet to say their last farewells, Rudy tugs on her father's arm in the midst of his eulogy and demands that she be allowed to go watch television.

Most children do not recover this quickly. Frequently, a child feels guilt – he believes he is responsible for the death either through neglect or through some mistake on his part. For instance, my son once had a cat who loved to jump into the bathtub. When the cat developed pneumonia and died, Jon moped around for days, finally "confessing" that once he had not waited for the cat to jump into the bath water, but had put it in the tub himself. When I assured him that pneumonia is a result of a virus, he was able to resolve his grief. A child may also blame others as well, a parent or a sibling, for not taking care of the pet properly.

In spite of Rudy's reaction, a child usually profits from staging a funeral. It is a *real* game through which he can work out his grief (Grollman 14), not unlike adult funerals, which provide the same comfort. Funeral arrangements include making a guest list, writing a proper eulogy, choosing a suitable grave site, marking the grave site, and perhaps serving refreshments afterwards. Disposing of a pet without the child present, while usually well-meant, may prevent the child from accepting the reality of death.

One of the most comforting and effective techniques is dwelling upon happy memories of the pet. E.V. Rieu's poem "Cat's Funeral" is a lovely piece of literature because of its vivid imagery, its effective diction, its sustained tone, but is probably inappropriate for most children. Because the poem emphasizes the loss—"No more to watch bird stir . . . No more to revel in milk . . ."—rather than the legacy of memories, it encourages the child to maintain his grief.

Another mistake parents frequently make is trying to replace the pet prematurely. Only when the child has gone through the proper process of grief will he be able to embrace a new pet, to transfer his love to a new object.

Most books dealing with the death of a pet appeal to a younger audience, children from three to eight. Those currently available do reflect, for the most part, natural reactions and proper handling of the loss.

Although Margaret Wise Brown's *The Dead Bird* is nearly fifty years old, it remains a classic for its simplicity and its wisdom. Four children come upon a dead bird. The physiological aspects of death are clear: the bird, its eyes closed, is still warm, but no heartbeat exists, and soon it grows cold and stiff. Even though the bird is not a pet, the children respond lovingly by burying it in the woods and having a funeral during which they sing a song, cover the grave with flowers, and put on a stone above the grave: "Here lies a bird that is dead." For days, they continue to visit the grave, placing new flowers on it and singing—until they forget. Life does go on.

Carol Carrick takes two books to cover the grief process. *The Accident*, a somber book, tells the story of Christopher and his dog, Bodger, who is killed when he runs in front of a pickup truck. The driver is not at fault, but Christopher vents his anger at the man. He is also angry at his father.

> He was hoping his father would find that it was all a mistake, that Bodger was going to be O.K. At least he wanted his father to get mad at this man and tell him he would be punished for

what he did. Instead, his father was agreeing with the man, feeling sorry for him. He didn't even care about Bodger.

That night in bed, Christopher indulges in the age-old game,
"What if?" He tries to pretend that the accident did not happen. He
also goes through the universal misery of awakening in the morning
and for a few moments not remembering reality, only to have all
the anguish come flooding over him. His father and mother try to
help, he by offering to take Christopher fishing, she by offering
French toast—with jelly. Unfortunately, his father, thinking he is
doing a kindness, has gone ahead and buried Bodger. Christopher,
of course, reacts violently. The father, however, realizes his mistake
and suggests that the two of them find a nice stone to mark Bodger's
grave. Christopher painstakingly searches for the right stone.
When they place it at the foot of the dog's grave, his father begins
reminiscing about Bodger, allowing the boy to treasure his
memories and to cry openly.

In the sequel, *The Foundling*, the author explores the replacement of a pet. Although Christopher befriends the puppy of his
neighbors, the Tiltons, he is not yet ready for a dog of his own. He
no longer has bad dreams, and he has stopped reliving the accident,
but he still wishes that Bodger were there. Thus when his father
takes him to the local animal shelter and shows him a puppy,
Christopher sadly turns down the chance to take the puppy home.
He worries that no one else will want the animal, but he would be
unfaithful to Bodger if he should get another dog so soon after the
loss of his beloved pet.

Confused and unhappy, Christopher rides to the town dock,
where he finds the Tiltons' puppy. He rescues the dog and takes it
to the Tiltons. To his amazement, they tell him that the puppy does
not belong to them, but is a stray. Suddenly, he decides that this
puppy he will keep and love.

Jamie, the central character of Sandol Warburg's *Growing Time*,
also loses his dog, King, who dies of old age. His family is almost
unbelievably understanding: His mother comforts him, cries for
King, and helps him plant flowers on King's grave; his Uncle John
reassures him that King will become part of the rich earth, helping
to feed "'all living growing things'" (10); Granny assures him that
King has not really gone away—"'That's only his poor worn-out

body that was a bundle of aches and pains to him. (22) . . . the spirit of something you really love can never die. It lives in your heart. It belongs to you always, it is your treasure'" (24). Nevertheless, Jamie must go through the necessary steps: He cannot eat, he pretends that King is still alive, and he keeps remembering all the special moments he shared with his pet.

When his mother and father immediately bring home a new puppy, Jamie is not yet ready for another pet and ignores his gift. That night, however, he has a lovely dream and awakes to rescue the puppy, who has had an accident in the kitchen. He is now ready to face life again. While the recovery is too swift to be believable, the book does follow the normal grief process.

A too-swift recovery mars an otherwise delightful book, Miriam Cohen's *Jim's Dog Muffins*. When Muffins is killed, Jim's classmates react predictably: "'Jim's dog got killed by the garbage truck! It was all squashed!'" "'Did Jim cry?'" The class writes him a letter, and all try to comfort him when he returns to school, but Jim can't concentrate on his work and lashes out at those who are simply trying to help. The teacher explains, "'Maybe Jim needs time to feel sad.'" But on the way home, his friend Paul asks him to go for pizza, and when Paul stuffs his pizza in his mouth, both begin to laugh and then to discuss Muffins. As they walk home, arms around each other's shoulders, we know that Jim is on his way to recovery.

Still another dog dies in Sarah Abbott's *The Old Dog*. When Ben wakes up and pats his dog, she does not respond. Ben's father tells him that the dog is dead. At first, Ben is not upset since the dog simply seems asleep: "Then it isn't bad to die, Ben thought. To die is to lie there as though you're sleeping." When he returns from school that afternoon, however, he realizes that the dog is truly gone, and he begins to cry. He reiterates all that has gone: "no wet tongue" to lick the tears away or "to comfort him" or "to welcome the black ball of a puppy Ben's father was bringing home." The book does a good job of emphasizing the finality of death and the loss one feels when a pet dies. Unfortunately, the book stresses the negative, the loss, rather than the positive, memories of the dog; and the replacement of the old dog with a new puppy is far too soon to be acceptable to the child.

Far more realistic is Tobi Tobias's *Petey*. When Emily finds her pet gerbil Petey huddled in the corner of his cage, she fears the worst. Her kind father explains that after all, Petey is five, "'pretty old for a gerbil.'" After reading a book on the care of pets, which tells them that a doctor will do no good, that Petey will either get well or die, they nevertheless try to give the animal medicine and try to feed him, but the gerbil does not respond. When Emily grows angry, her father explains that it is better for Petey to die quickly than to suffer a long sickness. Emily checks upon her pet during the night, but by the morning, he is dead. After a long conversation in which the entire family share memories of Petey, they bury him in the back yard.

Life goes on for Emily, but she still cannot forget Petey. She misses him particularly at night. When spring comes, a friend calls to say that her gerbil has had babies and that Emily may have one. Emily is not sure that she wants another gerbil. When she tells her mother that a new pet would not be the same, her mother says, "'I never said it would be the same. It can be different, Em, and still be good.'" When the book ends, Em has planned to think the matter over and let her mother know if she wants a new pet.

Stressing the healing power of fond memories is Edith Hurd's *The Black Dog Who Went Into The Woods*. When Black Dog goes into the woods and does not return, Benjamin, the youngest child, realizes that he has died. The others contradict him. Both Rose, the middle child, and Sam, the oldest, insist that he will come back. Even their mother and father are not ready to believe that Black Dog is really gone.

The entire family spend the day looking for their pet, but do not find him. The others continue to search as the week wears on, but not Benjamin. Finally, all agree that the dog is probably dead. "'I think,' Father said, 'that Benjamin understands better than any of us. Animals sometimes do go into the woods, or someplace, by themselves when they know it is time for them to die'" (14).

That night, beneath a full moon, Black Dog visits each one of the family members as they dream: Mother of their first getting Black Dog; Father of Black Dog barking at a deer and her two fawns; Sammy of running through the woods chasing chipmunks with Black Dog; Rose of swimming with Black Dog and later chastising him for shaking and covering her with water; and Benjamin of playing tug-of-war with Black Dog and then slipping his pet into bed with him. Each one wakens and thanks Black Dog for coming to say good-bye. In the morning, they all reveal that Black Dog visited them in the night. "Benjamin did not say anything more about Black Dog after that" (32).

Two books offer a more philosophical approach. When an old pet bird dies in Mildred Kantrowitz's *When Violet Died*, the children have an elaborate funeral. Several friends and neighbors bring gifts: a box to bury Violet in, a ribbon to tie the box, cotton balls to line it, and cornflower seeds to plant on the grave. One child reads a poem; another sings. Afterwards, all the guests have strawberry punch. It is the promise of this punch that keeps one guest, Billy, at the service. Adding some humor to the book, Billy complains that the funeral is boring and threatens to leave because of a sudden stomachache when he hears that one child is going to sing. Both Amy and Eva are depressed. Amy goes to her room after telling Eva that "'Nothing lasts forever . . . nothing.'" But Eva realizes that when Blanche the cat has her kittens, she will keep one and name her Blanche, and then the second Blanche will have kittens, and Eva will keep one and name *her* Blanche, and she rushes to tell Amy that ". . . maybe nothing lasts forever, but she knew a way to make it last a long, long time!"

Likewise *The Attic Treasure* by Steve McKinstry and Lucy Rigg is lovely because of its marvelous illustrations, each abounding with attractive, fascinating details. For instance, the attic scene shows old photographs, hat boxes, an old lantern, baskets, a rocking chair, old letters, books, a cradle, a doll buggy, and numerous toys no longer used—boats, a tea set, a hobby horse, a guitar. The only drawback is the use of bears as the main characters, a choice that does not detract from the book but that does not add to it either. Nevertheless, the subtle insights into death make it worthwhile.

Since spring has arrived, the family is doing spring housecleaning and getting rid of the junk accumulated over the year. As Lucy and Ben take items to the attic for storage, they discover old treasures. After donning some old clothes, they learn from their parents that the attic holds special memories for everyone—for instance, a picture of Mama, as a baby, with her parents. She says, "'When you love someone, you always miss them when they are gone. But you always have their memory, like this attic, where all the good things are stored. Whenever I want to be close to them again, I just shut my eyes and remember.'"

This insight is to come in handy, for the children find an injured bird whom they want to help but who dies by the next day in spite of all the ministrations of the family. Papa warns the children that the bird may not live, but they are determined to help. Benjamin even sneaks out of bed that night to stay by the bird in the attic. Benjamin is sad that the bird has died, upset that God has not taken care of Attie the bird. Even though they give Attie a funeral complete with a small bouquet of flowers and a prayer, Ben is not appeased. Later, his mother comforts him, explaining that "'When it was Attie's time to go, he wasn't alone, but with someone that would love and remember him.'"

When Ben asks if he will ever see the bird again, his mother advises him not to think of the future without Attie, but of the past when he had the bird to care about—"'That's a gift many of us never receive or appreciate fully.... Besides, there is a way you can be close. Remember what I told you about my Mama and Papa in the attic?'" Ben begins to feel better as he remembers Attie, seeing him fly through the sky and hearing him sing. Suddenly, he realizes that a bird really is singing, not Attie as he would have liked, but a mother bird welcoming three newborn birds. Thus Ben learns that life is cyclical, and while he does not have Attie, he can still appreciate the beauty of the world, can "watch the miracle of life taking place."

By far the best book in this category on the market today is Judith Viorst's *The Tenth Good Thing About Barney*. The first-person narration by a small boy whose cat, Barney, has just died gives the book its charm and emphasizes a child's reactions to the death of a pet. When the cat dies, not only does the boy cry, but he can't eat his dinner—not even his chocolate pudding. The parents are marvelous. His mother plans the funeral and asks her son to think of ten good things about Barney to recite about him. When he recites them, his mother assures him that they are wonderful, but she has counted only nine. Afterwards, he and his friend Annie argue over Barney's whereabouts, she insisting that Barney is in heaven, he that his cat is under the ground. Wisely, the father says that they both may be right, but adds, "'We don't know too much about heaven.... We can't be absolutely sure that it's there.'" Annie is undaunted. "'But if it is there,' said Annie in her absolutely sure voice/ 'it's bound to have room for Barney and tuna and cream.'"

When his father asks him to help in the garden and the child assents, "'but only a little'" because he doesn't like it that Barney is dead, the father assures him that his feelings are okay. He then explains that Barney, in the ground, will change and will help flowers and the tree and the grass to grow. Thus at bedtime, he repeats to his mother the nine good things about Barney and adds the tenth: "Barney is in the ground and he's helping grow flowers./ You know, I said, that's a pretty nice job for a cat."

While most of the books on the death of a pet are understandably aimed at a younger audience, older children suffer as well. *The Trouble with Thirteen* by Betty Miles is a presentation of typical and believable conflicts of a girl approaching her thirteenth birthday, principally revolving around her fear of approaching adulthood, and humor does appear in the book. The treatment of death, however, is somewhat superficial. First of all, Annie's dog, Nora, dies in an unconvincing manner. One night, the dog is wheezing, evidently having caught a cold. The next day, realizing that Nora hasn't greeted her after school, Annie finds the dog under a lilac bush. Not only does she not move the dog in from the rain, she does not even cover it, but simply cradles it in her arms. Within minutes, Nora dies: "She raised her head a little bit and laid it closer to mine so that our eyes looked into each other's. Then, thumping her tail softly as though she was trying to please me by doing a trick just right, she gave a little quick gasp, and died." This scene borders on sentimentality. Annie blames her father for not having taken the dog to the vet the night before, but quickly forgives him. The family relate fond memories of Nora, but the dialogue is stilted and unnatural. After a hurried funeral, life goes back to normal. True, occasionally Annie expresses her sadness, especially when her best friend, Rachel, moves away soon after Nora's death; but the reader cannot really feel her emotions.

A more realistic approach exists in John Donovan's *I'll Get There. It Better Be Worth the Trip*. David Ross meets the world with wonderful humor and incredible vulnerability. Until age thirteen, his life has been pleasant enough. Although his parents are divorced, his life with his maternal grandmother has been full of love, friendship, and freedom. Now his grandmother is dead. His loss is intense: "She worked very hard at being a good parent. She never had the pleasure of being a grandparent. Poor good girl. Now she never will" (13–14). Her most precious gift to him was Fred, a dachshund she presented him on his eighth birthday, his only friend now. And where will he live? In the days that follow, he visits his grandmother's grave every day, not wishing to leave her all alone, particularly through the winter, but he must go to New York to live with his mother, who reluctantly agrees that Fred will go as well.

David's life with his mother is far from blissful. The dog continues to upset her, she resents her responsibilities to David, her mood shifts are sudden and violent—and she is drunk most of the time. In addition, David must also deal with arranged visits with his father's new wife, Stephanie. David does begin to enjoy school, he learns to love Stephanie, and he makes a special friend, Altschuler, an independent, streetwise boy. Ultimately, their friendship becomes physical, causing undue problems. Although his mother only suspects what has happened, she places a hysterical phone call to his father and takes Fred for a walk so that Dave and his father can talk. Fred gets loose, is hit by a car, and dies. Not only is David unable to bear this loss, he feels ultimate guilt—"All that messing around. Nothing would have happened to Fred if I hadn't been messing around with Altschuler. My fault. Mine!" (144). He and Altschuler do finally make up and resolve to be friends again. But David has had too much to face for a child his age.

The Newbery Award–winning novel *Island of the Blue Dolphins* by Scott O'Dell follows the true story of a woman, the Lost Woman of San Nicolas, inadvertently left alone for eighteen years on an island seventy-five miles southwest of Los Angeles. Taking the few available facts, O'Dell has imagined her story, creating a compelling tale.

Death is a central part of the book. When the Aleuts visit the island to hunt otter, they renege on their deal with the tribe's chief, Karana's father, and a battle ensues, leaving many of the tribe dead, particularly the men. The remaining members eventually decide to leave the island. As the ship is leaving her harbor, however, Karana spots her younger brother Ramo still on shore and jumps overboard. The very next day, a pack of wild dogs kill Ramo, leaving Karana completely alone on the island. The remainder of the book covers her struggle for survival, which is also a compelling struggle against loneliness.

When the book begins, Karana and the other people of her tribe must deal with the loss of their husbands, fathers, brothers. Not only do their reduced numbers make the work difficult and cause tension, but their grief is ever-present. "Those who had died at Coral Cove were still with us. Everywhere we went on the island or on the sea . . . they were with us. We all remembered someone and I remembered my father. . . . It was the memory of those who had gone that burdened our hearts" (27–28).

Next she must face Ramo's death. Days pass full of inertia. Finally, Karana decides that she can no longer remain in the empty village; the memories are painful there, and so she burns it. Even though she begins to make a new home elsewhere on the island, she keeps alive Ramo's memory by vowing vengeance on the wild dogs, particularly their leader, the dog with the yellow eyes. She does kill two of them and seriously wounds the leader. Later, however, when she comes upon him, instead of finishing him off with another arrow, she automatically picks him up, carries him to her home, and nurses him back to health. Through a long, painstaking process, the two become best friends. As a result of this experience and the many others she has with other animals and birds who are her only companions, she vows never to kill again. "For animals and birds are like people, too, though they do not talk the same or do the same things. Without them the earth would be an unhappy place" (156).

Her island is certainly an unhappy place when Rontu (the dog) dies. Finding him weak and near death, Karana carries him home, and he dies the next day. Once again, inertia sets in. She manages to survive for two more years until a ship from America comes and rescues her. Although Karana will once more be around people, the ending is somewhat sad, for Karana has come to love her island, and she has suffered incredible loss.

In another Newbery book, William Armstrong's *Sounder*, death hovers throughout. During the late 1800's a black sharecropper and his family struggle to survive. None of the human characters have names; they are simply the boy, the father, the mother. Only Sounder, their coon dog, has a name. It is Sounder who not only helps provide food and companionship, but gives the family an identity. Otherwise, they are anonymous in a society that abuses them and ignores them. When the father, in desperation, steals a ham to feed the family, he is arrested. Sounder attacks the deputies who are carrying off his master and is severely wounded. The next day he has disappeared. The boy lives in constant fear – is Sounder dead? Is his father dead? The boy does visit his father once in the town jail, but after the sentencing, no one knows where the father is. Sounder does return eventually, horribly mutilated, but the father does not return for years, until he has been injured in an explosion and is thus no longer able to work.

While the primary themes deal with the injustices suffered by blacks and the boy's desperate yearning to read, the theme of death is important. Both Sounder and the father return only to die a short time later. The boy has learned to accept, however. He buries his father and prepares a grave for the dog, knowing that Sounder will not live long without his master. The boy has learned to read and finds comfort in the words of Montaigne: "'Only the unwise think that what has changed is dead.' He had asked the teacher what it meant, and the teacher had said that if a flower blooms once, it goes on blooming somewhere forever. It blooms on for whoever has seen it blooming" (112). Thus his father and Sounder are not really dead to the boy:

> Years later, walking the earth as a man, it would all sweep back over him, again and again, like an echo on the wind.
> The pine trees would look down forever on a lantern burning out of oil but not going out. A harvest moon would cast shadows forever of a man walking upright, his dog bouncing after him. And the quiet of the night would fill and echo again with the deep voice of Sounder, the great coon dog (113).

An equally realistic book, Marion Dane Bauer's *Shelter From The Wind*, is as much a celebration of life as it is a treatise on death. Running away from her father, her new stepmother Barbara, and the abhorrent thought of the new brother or sister on the way, Stacy heads for the Oklahoma panhandle, a barren, hostile land. After a grueling night, two German shepherd dogs find her and lead her to their mistress, Ella, living in isolation in a sandstone cabin her husband built for her in 1929.

It is Ella, in her no-nonsense fashion and in her practical acceptance of fate, who allows Stacy to come to terms with her life and to grow. During her stay with Ella, Stacy stops idealizing her real mother; she realizes that her mother was a drunk who deserted Stacy and her father, that Barbara makes her father happy. When

Stacy single-handedly must deliver the puppies of the German shepherd bitch, she discovers the true miracle of birth, and she begins to realize the joy of having children when Ella reveals that she lost three children and that perhaps her husband would not have deserted her if any of the children had lived.

The first puppy that Stacy delivers, the one who has difficulty being born and whose life she has saved, has a cleft palate, can't nurse, and will starve to death. Ella orders Stacy to drown the pup. Angry at Ella, who seems cold-hearted, angry at fate that she must kill the pup "born right into my hands" (90), she buries it and then, to cover the grave, in a wild frenzy almost strips bare Ella's wedding tree, a present treasured throughout the years and providing the only spot of beauty in Ella's life. In this act, she is venting her hatred not only of Ella, of Barbara, of life, but also of her mother. But Ella understands: "'A grave is a difficult thing to cover, Stacy'" (106). Worried, too, about Ella, who is old and vulnerable, Stacy suggests to Ella's neighbor that Ella should not be allowed to live by herself. He replies, "'So . . . that's her right, ain't it? To live the way she chooses—she's not hurting nobody out there. To die out there when the time comes'" (102–3).

Stacy is now ready to return to her home, ready to face the future, looking forward to the new baby and to the new puppy from the next litter that Ella has promised her.

The finest book available for an older reader is *A Day No Pigs Would Die* by Robert Newton Peck. This autobiographical work captures the innocence, the warmth, and the beauty of the author's childhood on a farm in Vermont. Even at age twelve, Robert has the realistic outlook on life common among farmers. The book begins with his harrowing struggle in helping a calf be born. He is basically comfortable with the propagation of animals. When a neighbor brings over a boar to mate with Pinky, Robert's pet pig, the scene is particularly violent; nevertheless, Robert understands that if Pinky remains barren, she is of no use to the family. His parents, too, see sex as a natural part of life. When Robert's Aunt Cassie complains to his mother that the Widow Bascom has taken up with her hired man, his mother defends the widow and accepts her behavior with a pragmatism that is refreshing: "'And if Iris Bascom and her man giggle in the dark, they can have my blessing for whatever it's worth'" (65).

Robert also accepts that animals must die so that others may live. His father, a gentle man, kills pigs as part of his livelihood – it is his job. When Robert sees a hawk kill a rabbit, he describes the rabbit's cry as "full of pity . . . I'd heard it once before, a rabbit's deathcry, and it don't forget very easy. . . . Maybe even a call for help, for somebody to come and end its hurting. It's the only cry a rabbit makes its whole life long, just that one deathcry and it's all over" (62). Then he matter-of-factly imagines the baby hawks feasting on this treat and envies them.

On the other hand, the family reject senseless violence. When a neighbor "weasels" a dog at their place, both father and son are appalled. A dog and a weasel are put in a barrel so that the dog will "'hate weasels in the future until her last breath. She'll always know when there's one around, and she'll track it to its hole, dig it out, and tear it up. A man who keeps a hen house got to have a good weasel dog'" (101). When Rob sees the condition of the dog afterwards, he insists that they kill it because it is in so much pain, and his father agrees, vowing never again to participate in such a barbaric practice. Robert comments to the dead dog: "'You got more spunk in you than a lot of us menfolk got brains'" (105).

Ultimately, Pinky the pig must die because she remains barren in spite of repeated attempts to breed her and because there is no meat for the winter. The boy can hardly bear the pain, and for a moment he hates his father. Then he sobs.

> I felt his big hand touch my face, and it wasn't the hand that killed hogs. It was almost as sweet as Mama's. His hand was rough and cold, and . . . I could see that his knuckles were dripping with pig blood. It was the hand that just butchered Pinky. He did it. Because he had to. Hated to and had to. And he knew that he'd never have to say to me that he was sorry. His hand against my face, trying to wipe away my tears, said it all. . . . I couldn't help it. I took his hand to my mouth and held it against my lips and kissed it . . . again and again. . . . So he'd understand that I'd forgive him even if he killed me (129–30).

Robert knows too that his father is going to die soon. His father has told him so and explained that Robert must be the head of the family when he is gone. When Haven Peck dies, Robert takes care of all the arrangements, participates in the funeral, and looks after his mother and his aunt. In his final farewell to his father, he says, "'Goodnight, Papa. We had thirteen good years'" (140). These thirteen years have left Robert with a priceless legacy: He knows how much he has always been loved, the guidance and training of his mother and father have left him prepared to meet the struggles he must endure through life, and he can embrace both life and death with the respect they both deserve.

III. The Death of a Friend

There was such speed in her little body,
And such lightness in her footfall,
It is no wonder that her brown study
Astonishes us all.

"Bells for John Whiteside's Daughter"
John Crowe Ransom

Less frequent than the death of a pet but usually more disturbing to a child is the death of a friend. Most books dealing with this subject appeal to children six years and older; during the earlier years, while a child may be temporarily disturbed when a friend dies, friendships at this age are not deep, and a lost friend is easily replaced. The only book currently available for younger children is an adaptation of a script from PBS's "Sesame Street." One of the show's writers, Norman Stile, composed this segment, "I'll Miss You, Mister Hooper," to explain the absence of Mr. Hooper, portrayed by Will Lee, who died in 1984. When Big Bird distributes pictures he has drawn as gifts for his adult friends, they tell him that Mr. Hooper has died. Like a child, he assumes that Mr. Hooper will return. When he learns differently, he immediately worries, "'Who's going to take care of his store? Who's going to make me birdseed milk shakes and tell me stories and . . . ?'" His other friends reassure him that they will take care of his needs. Still, Big Bird feels angry and sad. But Bob tells him, "'. . . We can be glad we had the chance to be with him and know him and love him when he was here.'" Even though Big Bird recalls some of his fondest memories of Mr. Hooper, he still is confused and demands one good reason for Mr. Hooper's dying. Gordon replies, "'It has to be this way...just because,'" an explanation many children can

46

understand because they, too, do things "just because." Big Bird hangs up Mr. Hooper's picture and says, "'I'll miss you, Mr. Hooper.'" Because the book deals with familiar and well-loved characters, it would appeal to most readers in spite of its heavy-handed approach. Two difficulties exist: The grief process takes only a matter of minutes, suggesting that one can recover immediately; and because Mr. Hooper is an adult, his death parallels that of a parent, not a friend.

Similarities do exist between the loss of a pet and the loss of a friend. Frequently, a child will deny the reality of the death. In both cases, the child may feel anger either at the loved one for dying or at another who the child feels must in some way be responsible. And in both cases, of course, the child must eventually express his grief, normally through an inability to handle normal routines such as eating and sleeping and later through tears. Finally, a child may also feel guilt over the death of a friend: He didn't do enough for his friend, or he did something to cause the death—or he didn't do enough to prevent the death. This last source of guilt points up one significant difference between the death of a pet and a friend. While pets and friends usually die as a result of an accident or an illness, friends may also kill themselves or be victims of murder (both increasing and alarming trends in our society). In any case, whatever the cause of death, the child, probably for the first time, realizes that he, too, may die. And if a friend has been murdered, deep-seated fears over one's own safety and security will emerge. Even if the murdered child is not a close friend, but simply a schoolmate, parents and teachers alike must provide support, guidance, and patience to help a child understand that yes, such tragedy *can* occur, but will most likely not happen.

Once again, children's books can help through their sensitive, realistic insights.

One of the most beloved books of all time, E.B. White's *Charlotte's Web*, stresses death throughout. Wilbur the pig is fated from the first page of the novel to face a major conflict with death. As a runt, he is not worth much, and thus Mr. Arable is going to kill him. Saved by Fern, Mr. Arable's daughter, Wilbur is nourished and then transferred to a neighboring farm only to learn that he is is to be turned into smoked ham and bacon at Christmas time. The novel is structured around this conflict. Once Wilbur learns of his doom, his friend Charlotte the spider makes four attempts to save him. By spinning in her web the words "Some Pig," then "Terrific," later "Radiant," and finally "Humble," she shows the world that Wilbur is no ordinary pig, that he deserves to live. When Wilbur wins a special prize at the fair, his future is secure.

The major themes of friendship, growth, and death intertwine to make this book a classic. As Wilbur matures, he learns the nature of friendship. Initially, his relationship with Charlotte is one-sided: She as an adult gives, and he as a child receives. By the end of the novel, however, Wilbur has learned to return these gifts. Wilbur must give up something in order to gain the help of Templeton the rat in retrieving Charlotte's egg sac after she dies, and he must assume the responsibility of raising Charlotte's children—and their children. He is ready to make these sacrifices: "'But you have saved me, Charlotte, and I would gladly give my life for you—I really would'" (164).

Wilbur must face not only the possibility of his own early death but the certainty of Charlotte's. White prepares the reader for this event throughout the book. When Wilbur first meets Charlotte and has doubts about her character, the reader learns that "underneath her rather bold and cruel exterior, she had a kind heart, and she was to prove loyal and true to the very end" (41). Later, we find that "Charlotte had worries of her own, but she kept quiet about them" (115). She warns Wilbur that she may not be able to accompany him to the fair. And "she knew that she couldn't help Wilbur much longer" (117). Finally, Charlotte helps Wilbur by showing her own acceptance of death and by giving him a positive direction in life.

> "You have been my friend," replied Charlotte. "That in itself is a tremendous thing. I wove my webs for you because I like you. After all, what's life anyway? We're born, we live a little while, we die. A spider's life can't help being something of a mess, with all this trapping and eating flies. By helping you, perhaps I was trying to lift up my life a trifle. Heaven knows anyone's life can stand a little of that" (164).

Charlotte's death scene is moving. Appropriately placed in the deserted fairgrounds, only hours before full of gaiety and laughter, the setting emphasizes the pathos. White is not sentimental, however; he does not dwell on the scene. The next chapter begins:

"And so Wilbur came home to his beloved manure pile in the barn cellar" (172). He anticipates the birth of Charlotte's babies and a long, happy life. Charlotte's natural acceptance of death and her insistence that one must live his life productively because life *is* short help him accept and go on. Even though Charlotte dies, her life has been worthwhile, and she has enriched Wilbur's existence:

> Wilbur never forgot Charlotte. Although he loved her children and her grandchildren dearly, none of the new spiders ever quite took her place in his heart. She was in a class by herself. It is not often that someone comes along who is a true friend and a good writer. Charlotte was both (184).

Although Wilbur is representative of a child, and most readers therefore easily identify with him, most of the books in this chapter deal with realistic characters. One outstanding book is *A Taste of Blackberries* by Doris Smith. This sensitive story tells of the grief the first-person narrator, a boy, undergoes when he loses his friend Jamie. Everyone likes Jamie even though he is a show-off and doesn't know when to quit. Thus when Jamie is stung by a bee and begins writhing on the ground, the narrator assumes that Jamie is still "putting on his act" and screams, "'You might as well quit it you brat. . . . Nobody's even watching you'" (19). When he finds out that Jamie was allergic to bees and has died, he feels horrible guilt. At first, he tries to deny reality:

> That Jamie! He was an expert attention getter, even when, maybe, he didn't intend to be. I wondered briefly if he had been faking unconsciousness just to keep from grinning at all of us. It would serve him right if he was out cold and didn't even know he was riding in an ambulance (26).

And when his mother tells him the truth he feels "trapped. I didn't want to listen to her telling me lies about Jamie" (28). But when he realizes what has happened,

> It was as though she had punched me in the stomach. I saw Jamie again, falling down and writhing. I closed my eyes. I shouldn't have left. I should have helped him. But how could I know? I swallowed. I thought I was going to be sick" (28).

He continues this charade, at first refusing to go to the funeral because by doing so, he would have to admit that his best friend is dead. When he finally sees Jamie, he must admit the truth; desperately, he runs from the funeral home. The boy's father catches him and hugs him, but the boy is not able to cry until that night in bed when his father holds him.

The next day the boy journeys into the yard of his neighbor, Mrs. Mullins. When he asks her why Jamie had to die, she replies, "'Honey, one of the hardest things we have to learn is that some questions do not have answers.' ... This made more sense than if she tried to tell me some junk about God needing angels" (43). And when he asks what it is like to be dead, she assures him that it is another one of those questions.

The boy is unable to eat until after the funeral. The funeral itself is simply a series of impressions—flowers, music, a droning of words, and at the cemetery, he doesn't pay much attention. "During the prayer, I looked at the toes of my shoes. It was hard to think about God when something as small as a bee could kill your best friend" (51).

The next day, the boy wishes to go play but feels that he would be wicked to do so. Instead, he goes to pick blackberries, a special pleasure he and Jamie shared. He takes the berries to Jamie's mother, his attempt to show her that he cares, that he will be there for her. When she says to him, "'I'll bake a pie. And you be sure to come slam the door for me now and then'" (56), he knows she understands everything he wanted to tell her, and he realizes that the main sadness is over.

Equally appealing and insightful is Eve Bunting's *The Empty Window*. Here, the main character, C.G., must desperately cope with the impending death of his friend Joe who lives downstairs in their inner-city apartment house. C.G. has overheard Joe's mother telling his mother that Joe has simply a few more days to live. Although C.G. has not seen Joe for weeks—he has refused to visit his friend—he does know that Joe has been fascinated with a group of parrots nesting in a neighborhood tree, indeed, that Joe spends hours at his window looking at the colorful birds. Thus C.G. and his younger brother Sweeny make a last desperate attempt to capture one of the parrots, the one C.G. has named Tag-Along because it seems an outsider.

The limited time C.G. has to give his friend his gift and the harrowing capture of the parrot, involving a terrifying climb and deep wounds where the parrot bites C.G., add tremendous suspense to the book. The main value, however, lies in C.G.'s visit to his friend. Instead of simply leaving the parrot as he has hoped to do, C.G. is pressured into giving it to Joe himself. And he is petrified. He has heard that Joe has lost all his hair (presumably from chemotherapy), he is embarrassed by the tears in Joe's father's eyes, he is ashamed of his opening question, "'Is Joe in?'" – of all the dumb things I could have said, this must be the dumbest." Mostly, he is afraid of the way Joe will look –

> He'll look the way he does in my nightmares, with a skeleton head and a skeleton smile. He's not like me anymore. He's not like anyone. He's dying.

And he worries, "What do you say to someone who's dying? You can't say, 'The Dodgers look good this year.'"

C.G. is in for a real surprise. Joe really doesn't look that different; his hair is simply shorter. And they do talk about the Dodgers. Most importantly, Joe refuses the parrot; he wants to let it go:

> "...because it is wild and free. That's why I like them, C.G. I watch them and I think about things. Like when we climbed up into Eaton Canyon that time and sat in the tree, and it was so windy".

Suddenly, C.G. understands:

> I look at Joe, and the whole of him is straining toward the sweep of the birds and his body is pulling, trying to get outside of itself.

C.G. gladly releases the bird.

After talking a bit more to his friend, C.G. leaves with plans to visit again the next day. He "would have, too, but Joe died that night." C.G. cries a bit as he watches the parrots the next evening and realizes that he is not crying for Joe:

> Maybe I was crying because the parrots are so beautiful and Joe isn't here to see them, and because in the apartment two floors below me, the window is shining and empty. . . . The most awful thought has come into my head, and it's worse than awful because I know it's true. I'd wanted to get Joe a parrot to keep him company so I wouldn't have to.

The ending of the book poignantly shows the reader that someone who is dying is not to be feared, and that we must not waste one precious minute with those we love.

Sam Greene, the narrator of *Thank You, Jackie Robinson* by Barbara Cohen, must also say good-bye to a friend. Remembering the years when he was "Nuttier than a fruitcake. Madder than a hatter. Out of my head" (7), Sam reveals that the death of his father when Sam was seven had created definite personality quirks, some of them serious. First of all, he is a loner, not completely by choice. Because his mother runs an inn two miles out of town, he has no neighbors, and the distance prevents him from joining in activities with other boys his age. In addition, his mother is constantly busy, his two younger sisters, close in age, depend upon each other, and his older sister Sara reads ten books a week, content to remain in her own world. His isolation is also self-imposed because he fears contact with strangers. Sam lacks self-worth; he refers to himself as a "scrungy, freckled-faced little Jewish kid" who gets "picked last for the teams" (10).

To compensate for his loneliness, he becomes obsessed with the Brooklyn Dodgers, eventually being able to relate, at will, any game in its entirety from the 1940s on. When his mother hires a new cook, Davy, who shares Sam's passion for the Dodgers, a long-lasting friendship begins.

Davy serves two key functions in the book. As the friendship develops, he assumes the role of a father to Sam, taking him to ball games, fixing him special breakfasts, passing on valuable insights into life. At the same time, because Davy is black, the author is able to raise the consciousness of her readers so that they can understand the devastation racism can cause and can begin to empathize with people suffering this discrimination. The most poignant scene occurs when Sam sees a runner deliberately try to spike Jackie Robinson, the first black in baseball. When Sam questions Davy about the incident, Davy replies, "'It's just one of the things the first Negro in baseball has got to put up with'" (44), and when Sam says, "'That doesn't seem right,'" Elliot, Davy's son-in-law, replies, "'There ain't nothing right about this whole damn life!'" (44).

The friendship continues until Sam's twelfth year, when Davy falls ill and is hospitalized. Hints of the seriousness of his heart condition appear throughout the book. However, when Davy's daughter Henrietta continuously nags Davy about his health, Davy finally blurts out: "'Listen, Henrietta, if you have to go around all the time taking it easy, you might as well be dead'" (54). Even though Sam admires his friend's courage, he is desperate to see him, to do something for him, but only the immediate family may visit. At this point, the reader learns that Sam has never truly recovered from his father's death. "'It's a good thing I'm twelve now. They'll let me in. They would never let me in when Dad was sick. Not until that last day, anyway'" (67). The author here shows that parents and hospital authorities do great harm when they separate children from parents who are terminally ill.

Finally, Sam devises a plan. Through hoarding and eventually borrowing money, he gets to Ebbets Field. After a series of adventures and misadventures, he is able to tell his story to Jackie Robinson, who agrees to have all the members of the team sign a baseball for Davy. This accomplishment is particularly important in Sam's development, for in trying to give to his friend Davy, he must conquer his fear of strangers.

After Elliot manages to sneak Sam into the hospital and Sam first sees Davy, "such a small lump under that white sheet for a man who a few weeks before must have weighed more than two hundred pounds" (102), Sam wants to run away. Afterwards, he realizes that there "was no magic in the ball. He [Davy] loved it but there was no magic in it. It was not going to cure him, the way deep down in my heart I had somehow thought it would" (110). When he goes home that night, he cries himself to sleep. A week later, Davy dies.

As a Jewish boy, Sam is unprepared for the Christian funeral. He had wanted to attend his father's funeral, but his mother would not let him or Sara go. Sara had:

> . . . felt that she had been pushed away from what really was important that day, as if somehow our father's death wasn't sup-

posed to matter to her, or as if Mother didn't want her around.... I guess Mother had decided not to make the same mistake twice (112).

But Sam doesn't care about having missed his father's funeral and doesn't want to go to this one. Forced to view the body of his friend, Sam blurts out, "'That isn't Davy'" (114). Henrietta is insulted, but Elliot explains, "'That's just Davy's shell, there in the box'" (115). Further, because the Jewish religion does not stress an afterlife, Sam is unable to accept Henrietta's explanation that her father "'...is sitting on the right hand of Jesus this very minute'" (115). Later, in the car with his mother, Sam says that it's not fair for both his father and his friend to have died. His mother stresses that he shall always have memories of David, but Sam remains bereaved, "I thought the emptiness I felt where I was supposed to have a heart was never going to go away" (117).

After the funeral, Sam retreats to his room, refusing even to listen to a baseball game. When his mother joins him, she warns, "'Don't feel too sorry for yourself for too long.... It doesn't pay. Take if from one who knows'" (120). Sam is angry at his mother's interference and wishes that she had lied to him that she was sure Davy was in heaven, even though he knows he wouldn't believe her. He continues to think about the game, but feels

> ... that to turn on that radio would have been some kind of betrayal of the love, and the anger, and the grief I had been feeling all week—all the emotions which I thought I'd have been better off if I'd never known, and yet which I stubbornly clung to as if I'd cease to exist once they ceased to exist (122).

Realizing "maybe, just maybe that Davy was somewhere—somewhere else" (123), he turns on the radio and cheers Jackie Robinson on: "'Hit it for Davy, Jackie. Hit it for your friend Davy'" (124). Sam, older now, says that he will always be able to see Jackie Robinson, "running from base to base in a brand-new baseball game that will never, ever be over" (124).

By far the best book on the death of a friend is Katherine Paterson's Newbery book, *Bridge to Terabithia*, centering around the friendship of ten-year-old Jess and Leslie Burke, a newcomer to rural Virginia. Before Leslie's arrival, Jess's life is dismal. Three of his four sisters torment him—the two older, Brenda and Ellie, with their selfishness and self-absorption, the youngest, Joyce Ann, with her whining; he is close only to May Belle. His mother, worn by worry and poverty, simply nags him. Most of all, he feels alienated from his father, who gives Jess little attention and who is contemptuous of Jess's need to paint. Lacking self-worth, full of doubts, and obsessed with many fears, Jess is in dire need of Leslie. She, too, will suffer. Because of her unconventional dress, her parents' values (they do not even own a television set), her independence, she does not receive acceptance or approval. The two, however, create their own kingdom, Terabithia, where they can reign supreme, where all the terrors of the world disappear.

The friendship flourishes, Jess is receiving encouragement for his art work through a perceptive teacher, and Jess is finally learning to like himself and to cope with his world. Unfortunately, tragedy strikes. Instead of meeting Leslie at the creek to cross over to their special place, he accepts a last-minute invitation to go to Washington, D.C., for the day with his music teacher, Miss Edmonds. Not only is he thrilled that he can visit an art museum, but he is also relieved, for the day is stormy, and he has dreaded swinging across the creek, water being one of his more pressing fears. At the end of the day, he ironically thinks, "This one perfect day of his life was worth anything he had to pay" (101).

As he enters his home, he realizes that something is amiss. His sister blurts out, "'Your girlfriend's dead, and Momma thought you was dead, too'" (102). Not realizing that Jess had gone to Washington, his parents think that Jess has also drowned when they hear about Leslie's death. Jess cannot comprehend and quickly turns to denial. Madly, he takes off running, "knowing somehow that running was the only thing that could keep Leslie from being dead. It was up to him. He had to keep going" (104). After his father picks him up in the truck and he returns home, Jess immediately falls asleep. As he awakens in the middle of the night, he still believes that all the horror has simply been a dream. Then he feels guilt that he didn't ask Leslie to go to Washington and determines to apologize to her in the morning.

That morning everything has changed. His father has done Jess's chores, and his mother has made him pancakes, a rare treat. As he downs pancake after pancake, his family is puzzled. The older girls taunt him, but his parents seem to understand that Jess has not admitted the truth. Gently they inform him that they must go pay their respects to the Burkes. Slowly, he begins to accept. Suddenly, he realizes that he will be important:

> He was the only person his age he knew whose best friend had died.... The kids at school ... would ... treat him with respect.... He wouldn't have to talk to anybody if he didn't want to, and all the teachers would be especially nice to him (112–3).

When Leslie's father talks to him, Jess becomes angry. "*You think it's so great to make everyone cry and carry on. Well it ain't*" (113). But it is not until Mr. Burke tells Jess that Leslie has been cremated that Jess realizes she is gone.

> How could they dare? Leslie belonged to him. More to him than to anyone in the world. No one had even asked him. No one had even told him. And now he was never going to see her again, and all they could do was cry.... He, Jess, was the only one who really cared for Leslie. But Leslie had failed him. She went and died just when he needed her the most. She went and left him (114).

In rage and despair, he runs home. May Belle, greeting him at the door, asks excitedly, "'Did you see her laid out?' He hit her. In the face. As hard as he had ever hit anything in his life" (115). Then he grabs the paints Leslie had given him for Christmas, runs to the creek, and flings them in. His father is there to comfort him, pulling Jess onto his lap and letting his son cry out his pain. "'I hate her. I wish I'd never seen her in my whole life,'" Jess says, and his father replies, "'Hell, ain't it'" (116). Now Jess has another problem. Because Leslie was not religious, Jess's fundamentalist background makes him fear that Leslie will go to hell. Once again, his father comforts him. "'Lord, boy, don't be a fool. God ain't gonna send any little girls to hell'" (116). Exhausted, Jess returns home. He wants to apologize to May Belle, but he is simply too weary. Later, Leslie's father brings to Jess P.T., the dog that Jess had given to Leslie for Christmas. That night, he is allowed to sleep with the dog.

The next morning Jess goes to Terabithia to pay his last respects to his friend. Typically, he begins to think of his own mortality; his sore throat seems ominous. "He didn't want to die. Lord, he was just ten years old. He had hardly begun to live" (119). He forces himself to swing across the creek and is making a wreath for Leslie when he hears May Belle screaming in fear. Halfway across the tree bridge spanning the creek, she has panicked. As he rescues her, he realizes that he has conquered his fear of water and reassures May Belle, "'Everybody gets scared sometimes, May Belle. You don't have to be ashamed'" (123).

When he returns to school, he is immediately ashamed that he "might be regarded with respect by the other kids. Trying to profit for himself from Leslie's death" (124). Amazingly, Mrs. Myers, his teacher, whom he has always considered an ogre, gives him words of comfort, her eyes full of tears, assuring him that he will never forget Leslie. And he realizes what Leslie has done for him.

> It was Leslie who had taken him from the cow pasture into Tera-bithia and turned him into a king. . . . Now it occurred to him that perhaps Terabithia was like a castle where you come to be knighted. After you stayed for a while and grew strong, you had to move on. For hadn't Leslie, even in Terabithia, tried to push back the walls of his mind and make him see beyond to the shin-ing world—huge and terrible and beautiful and very fragile?" (126).

Armed with this knowledge and ready to face the world, he now wishes to pass on this vision. He goes to Terabithia with May Belle to crown her the new queen.

While children before junior high need most guidance in cop-ing with the death of a friend, older children are by no means im-mune to agony. Irene Hunt's *Up a Road Slowly*, a Newbery winner, is permeated with death. Initially, seven-year-old Julie Trilling must face the death of her mother. Grieving for her mother and still recovering from the illness that struck them both, she is suddenly transported to her Aunt Cordelia's home to live, thus leaving behind her beloved older sister Laura and her father. Aunt Cor-delia is to present one of Julie's major conflicts, for the two have always "bristled" at one another. Aunt Cordelia seems inflexible and stern to Julie, Julie frivolous to Aunt Cordelia. Eventually, the two learn not only to live with one another, but to love and respect one another.

In the meantime, Julie must constantly face the loneliness brought about by her many losses: She misses her mother, her father, Laura, and her older brother, Chris, who has been sent away to school. When Laura marries and Julie goes on a visit, Julie expects no change in their relationship. However, Laura is pregnant: "I was not prepared to see her swollen grotesquely, her bright hair a little dulled, all the fresh radiance changed to a kind of pallid weariness" (41). Moreover, Bill, Laura's husband, becomes a rival: "They were both deeply involved in his work, very close and happy, very much like two people welded into a single unit" (42). The greatest outrage occurs when Julie realizes that she and Laura will not share the same bed, will not stay up late into the night talking and giggling. After Julie comes to grips with this problem, realizing that she cannot be number one in everyone's life, she must face the remarriage of her father. While Julie loves and admires her stepmother, Alicia, she once again feels cast aside. Later, she must also face the death of Mrs. Eltwing, a family friend, and the death of her Uncle Haskell, an aging, hypocritical alcoholic. Through Julie's strength of character and through Aunt Cordelia's wise, loving guidance, Julie meets each of these challenges and emerges victorious.

The most poignant part of the book concerns the death of a classmate. After Julie moves in with Aunt Cordelia, she attends the one-room school where Aunt Cordelia teaches. Also in the class is Aggie, "a mistreated, undernourished, and retarded girl, the youngest child of a shiftless, vicious father and a mother who had been beaten down by the cruelties of her life" (24). When Aggie discovers that Julie is Aunt Cordelia's niece, she becomes Julie's adoring fan. However, Julie is not amused.

> ...it was not Aggie's retardedness that made her a pariah among us; it was the fact that she stank to high Heaven. Aunt Cordelia had pled with the girl for years to treat herself to an occasional tub of soapy water, to shampoo her hair, to wash just once in a while the shabby dress which she wore every day of the year. Aggie would grimace and mouth some half-intelligible garble, but she never lost any of her over-ripe fragrance (24-5).

As a result, Julie, clever and resourceful – and cruel as children can sometimes be – abuses Aggie. For instance, she invents a game at lunch in which each day one girl is elected queen to sit in the middle of a circle, the others all with their backs to her. Aggie is always the queen. On Julie's tenth birthday, when Aunt Cordelia insists that Aggie be invited, Julie cancels the party.

When Aggie falls ill, Aunt Cordelia's insistence upon fairness requires that Julie visit Aggie.

> Aggie was lying on a bed in the corner of the room. It was a filthy bed, sheetless and sagging in the middle, and Aggie rolled restlessly upon it, her mouth parched with fever and her eyes glazed and unseeing. The heat, the stench, and the closeness of death made the place so unbearable that I wanted nothing so much as to break away and run from it.... Aggie was as indifferent to my presence as if I'd been one of the houseflies crawling along the edge of a spoon that lay on the table beside a bottle of medicine.... If I could have kept Aggie from dying by ignoring the stench and the ugliness, it would have been such an easy thing to do; it would have been a privilege to put my cheek next to hers and to tell her that yes, I was her friend. But Aggie would not look at me. . . . (50–1).

When Aggie dies and Aunt Cordelia, having helped prepare the body for burial, reveals that Aggie's hair, washed at last, was pretty, Julie reflects, "I wished that Aggie could have known. It seemed such a terrible waste – ugliness all one's life and something pretty discovered only after one was dead" (63).

Most children in their school years know an Aggie, a child who is poor or retarded. And most give into the temptation of teasing or taunting the unfortunate child who cannot fight back. When Julie's "victim" dies, she feels an enormous remorse. When she reveals her guilt to Uncle Haskell, he wisely says, "'You know very well that if this Kilpin girl could approach you again, as moronic and distasteful as she was a month ago, that you'd feel the same revulsion for her. You couldn't help it'" (66). Julie reluctantly agrees: "He was right of course. I thought how awkward it would be to have to say, 'Oh, Aggie, you were so nice when you were dead, and now you are here – the same old mess again.' That wouldn't do, naturally; one couldn't say *that*, even to Aggie" (66). Uncle Haskell sums up the message: "'. . .death may be the great equalizer; let's not give in to the hypocrisy that it is the great glorifier'" (66).

Thus Julie learns that one cannot truly grieve over the death of everyone, and that we cannot glorify the dead. But Uncle Haskell also explains, "'Guilt feelings do nothing for either you or the Kilpin child. But your compassion as you grow into womanhood may well become immortality for the girl you call Aggie'" (67–8).

Dave, in *Facing Up* by Robin F. Brancato, does lose his best friend. Dave is conservative and conventional, as are his parents. Although he has normal disagreements with them over curfew, mealtime, and the purchase of a car, he nevertheless respects them and does appreciate them. Jep, on the other hand, is wild and reckless. Because his parents are divorced and his mother frequently gone, he is left to his own devices, which include smoking, drinking and sex. Problems arise when Susan, Jep's girlfriend, makes a play for Dave. Although he feels tremendous guilt, Dave is love-struck, and for a period of weeks, he meets her separately. While the reader sees Susan for what she is – a vain, superficial girl who thrives on secrets and turmoil – Dave is blinded by love and lust.

Finally, disgusted both with her and with his own duplicity, Dave breaks off the relationship and vows to tell Jep the truth. A series of circumstances, however, prevents the disclosure. When Jep learns of the affair from Susan, he gets drunk and confronts Dave, swinging at his friend in anger, then passing out. As the three are on their way home, an accident occurs. Susan and Dave are not badly hurt, but Jep is killed. What follows is an excellent portrayal of the effects of grief when one loses a friend.

Specifically, Dave feels guilt: for having betrayed his friend, for not having told him the truth, for perhaps causing the accident. Dave cannot be sure that he was not at fault, although the police and the courts find him innocent of any wrongdoing.

As a result, Dave withdraws totally from his friends and his family. His only solace lies in reading and in working at his part-time job. Any reminder of Jep is painful. Finally, deceiving both his family and his friends, he sets off on a pilgrimage: He will go ahead with the vacation he and Jep had planned to take. A series of misadventures follows: miserable, rainy weather, the loss of his money, constant hunger, and near drowning. Having swum out too far in the lake, Dave cannot get back to shore. One part of him wants to drown—"He never meant to, but now that it's this way, let it be. His life for Jep's. Evens things up, right?... It's out of his hands" (165). Miraculously, the waves deposit him, unconscious, on the beach.

When he reaches the road and a state trooper finds him, Dave learns that his friends, Nan and Willo, have figured out where he was going and are at a nearby hotel. When he is able to spill out his heart to Nan, he is on the road to recovery. And she wisely suggests that he talk to his parents as well, basically kind and loving people who want to help. Dave knows that the pain will always follow him, but that he has the rest of his life to atone for his former mistakes, to "do something good now to balance the bad" (182).

Lynn, the protagonist of Susan Beth Pfeffer's *About David*, also loses her best friend in a tragic way. David, a high school senior, shoots his parents and then commits suicide. The focus of the book is the devastating effect suicide has on the survivors. We follow Lynn's agony from the immediate shock and grief through her tortuous attempts to understand and thus come to grips with David's actions. Although the dialogue is sometimes stilted, the author does an admirable job of exploring this perhaps most difficult kind of death to accept.

Lynn's overriding reaction, the one most typical to suicide, is guilt: Why didn't she see what was about to happen? Lynn cannot remember her lunchtime discussion with David on the last day of his life. She is sure that he had said something to indicate his intentions, and she is convinced that her essential responsibility and her resulting guilt are causing this memory lapse. Eventually, because she is not recovering as well as she should, her parents guide her to a psychiatrist. Finally, she is able to remember the conversation and to see that she probably could not have prevented the tragedy.

Other problems she faces are recurring nightmares, an inability to react socially with others, and anger at David for causing so much pain. The reader also sees the effect David's suicide has on his schoolmates. The most interesting insight is that time is necessary for one to pass through the grief cycle. While her family and friends become impatient with her—"'I'm just sick of it all,' she said, 'the way Lynn goes on, like she had a monopoly on suffering'" (131)—a new boy in school realizes that Lynn can't simply put the tragedy behind her, that she must deal with it in her own time and in her own way.

In dealing with David's suicide, the author tells of his problems—his insecurity as a result of having been adopted, his hatred for his adopted parents who demand perfection from him, his dismay because he thinks his mother is pregnant and thus he will be even more unloved—but these do not explain his ultimate act. Most people can learn to accept suicide, but few can fully understand it.

Another book that deals only tangentially with the death of a friend, *The Mimosa Tree* by Vera and Bill Cleaver, is nevertheless helpful in showing the amazing resilience of human beings and their will to survive even in the most difficult circumstances. The two main characters, Marvella and Hugh, move with their blind father, their stepmother, Zollie, and three younger brothers from their ramshackle farm in North Carolina to the slums of Chicago. There, any number of problems beset them. Zollie, seemingly warmhearted and fond of them all, simply does not come home one night. Marvella, finally able to find a part-time job working for a pawn broker, must quit when the welfare authorities learn she is only fourteen. Unfortunately, the bureaucrats in the welfare system, burdened with red tape and a totally impossible workload, fail to supply any help to the family. Finally, both Hugh and Marvella must resort to stealing in order for the family to survive their ordeal.

The children learn to steal with two neighborhood boys as instructors, boys who are streetwise and treacherous. Their portrayal is ambiguous—as it should be. While the children soon learn that the two, Frank and Mario, are not to be trusted, that they are deceitful and greedy, nevertheless some compassion for the two emerges. The reader sees their dismal existence: poverty and uncaring parents. And Frank does have genuine concern for his friend Mario, who is epileptic and who needs proper medical care. Indeed, some of the money Frank steals provides nourishing food for Mario and a visit to the doctor. When he accumulates enough money and they do go to a doctor, during the two-hour wait for his turn, Mario becomes disgusted and walks out, realizing the futility of the visit:

"It's *my* epilepsy. I don't have to have it treated if I don't want to. This doctor won't know how anyway. You know what he'll do? He'll ask me what seems to be the trouble. I'll tell him I got epilepsy. He'll feel my head. He might even X-ray it. Then he'll say, 'You got epilepsy. You should go to the country and live and take medicine every day and eat good'" (90).

Angry and disappointed, Frank turns on his friend in a rage. Mario has a seizure and dies on the street.

In the end, ashamed of themselves, Marvella and Hugh make the ultimate decision: They will return to the farm. When Frank hears they are leaving, he causes a scene and begs to go with them. Marvella thinks, "Somebody should help him. . . . But it can't be me. I don't know how. I don't know enough. I would have to undo all that's been done to him and I just wouldn't know how" (119).

Mature beyond their years, stripped of all childhood innocence, the two manage to get the family back to their home. There, the Critchers, formerly enemies, rush to greet them, bringing food and love and welcome. Marvella cries—"for all that had been found and lost in Chicago" (125).

A simple little tale by O. Henry, *The Last Leaf*, also stresses the joy of living, no matter what the circumstances. A young artist, Johnsy, develops pneumonia and becomes convinced that she shall die. The doctor realizes that she has lost the will to live, but tells her roommate, Sue, that Johnsy will live if she shows some sign of wanting to live. "'But whenever my patient begins to count the carriages in her funeral procession I subtract 50 per cent from the curative power of medicines. If you will get her to ask one question about the new winter styles in cloak sleeves I will promise you a one-in-five chance for her, instead of one in ten'" (15–16).

When Sue brings her paints to the sick room to try to cheer up her friend, she finds Johnsy morbidly counting the leaves on an ivy vine on the window as they drop to the ground, convinced that when the last leaf falls, she, too, will die.

Sue reveals her troubles to an upstairs neighbor, old Mr. Behrman, a crusty old man who is nevertheless caring. He replies:

"Is dere people in de world mit der foolishness to die because leafs dey drop off from a confounded vine? I haf not heard of

such a thing.... Vy do you allow dot silly pusiness to come in
der brain of her? Ache, dot poor leetle Miss Yohnsy" (22).

As Johnsy withdraws more and more into herself, almost willing herself to die, the November weather worsens. Surprisingly,
however, the last leaf stubbornly clings to the vine. Finally, Johnsy
realizes:

> "I've been a bad girl.... Something has made that leaf stay there
> to show me how wicked I was. It is a sin to want to die. You may
> bring me a little broth now, and some milk with a little port in
> it, and—no; bring me a hand-mirror first, and then pack some
> pillows about me, and I will sit up and watch you cook" (24–6).

The next day, Mr. Behrman dies. Sue tells Johnsy and then
reveals the cause of his pneumonia: "'Ah, darling, it's Behrman's
masterpiece—he painted it there the night that the last leaf fell'"
(28). In painting the leaf on the window, in waiting for Johnsy to
regain her will to live, Behrman has sacrificed his own life, pointing
out both the need of one to rejoice in life, to cling to it as long as
possible, and the obligation one has in life to care about others.

No matter what kind of loss one endures, it is memories of the
loved one that help us to survive. Such is the subject of Eric
Rhodin's *The Good Greenwood*. Told in first person by Mike, a high
school senior, the story alternates between a one-week period in the
present and flashbacks of the same time period a year before,
creating a mystery about the death of Louis, Mike's best friend. It
is not until the last pages of the book that the reader discovers the
details of the accidental self-inflicted wound that killed Louis.

While we assume that Mike has gone through the conventional
stages of grief, he still faces a major problem. His remembrance of
the real Louis is nebulous, fading like a face in an old photograph.
He needs to keep "remembering for sure the way it really was" (121).
Compounding the problem, actually causing the problem, are
others who knew Louis. Louis was a real slob, usually sporting a
floppy hat and a stretched-out, faded blue sweater; Mike's father
remembers him as "neat as a pin." Although Louis was a half-
hearted student, the Spanish teacher remembers that he had a true
flair for the language. Even though Louis in his last football game

missed a pass, the coach remarks: "'That Louis . . . would have been one of the few really good ballplayers we get around here'" (119). And the director of the social club even says that Louis had natural grace and skill even though Mike remembers, "He didn't seem to catch on to the music. . . . It was as if he was listening to some other time, so that he was always mixed up and clumsy" (25). No wonder Mike is confused.

Equally upsetting to him is that no one seems to remember the real Louis—a natural clown and a true poet, skimming through life with enthusiasm and imagination, endearing himself to everyone.

The adults in Mike's life are not ogres; in fact, Mike has a pleasant, honest, open relationship with all of them. But because their distorted memories of Louis cause him distress, Mike's behavior becomes somewhat bizarre. Specifically, in an attempt to make others remember Louis as he was, Mike begins wearing Louis's old sweater and cap. His charade creates problems. At first, the adults think they are seeing a ghost; they later realize that it is Mike they are seeing and fear he is becoming disturbed.

The entire novel revolves around the concept of vision. Mike finally realizes that others' concepts of Louis will not change.

> If someone is blind, there's not much use giving him a flashlight. He needs an operation or new eyes or something. . . . They were taking the *real* Louis's eyes . . . Louis's *real* voice . . . all those *real* ideas Louis had, like going over on the cliffs to look for the place where rabbits live or where rainbows get started, and they were sticking them in a trash bag (120–1).

Mike knows now that he will always remember the real Louis, and he can put his grief to rest.

Two books on the death of a friend definitely are appropriate only for older readers. Anyone familiar with Judith Guest's *Ordinary People* will find Patricia Windsor's *The Summer Before* reminiscent. Alexandra, or Alex, the protagonist, has not tried to kill herself, but she has been in a mental institution. During the first part of the novel, "The Winter After," she is in the process of recovery. We see the tension in her household: her parents' worry and resultant overprotectiveness, Alex's confusion and resentment of them. We find in Part Two, "The Summer Before," the cause of her mental and emotional problems. The relationship between Alex and Bradley, a friend since childhood, blossoms into a romantic one; they are truly in love. Unfortunately, her parents try to keep them apart, and when the two have been seen swimming nude, both sets of parents are furious. Alex is to be sent away to camp. Instead, she sneaks out and runs off with Bradley. The two eventually end up in a commune, one that falls far short of the ideals it represents. When one woman, obviously seriously ill but deprived of proper medical help, must be taken to the hospital, Bradley and Alex leave with another member, a wild, irresponsible man. On their flight, the car wrecks, and Alex watches Bradley burn to death. In the third part, "A Spring That Feels Like Autumn," we see Alex finally coming to terms with Bradley's death and making the first positive steps toward recovery.

The book is certainly intended for a more mature reader because of its frankness about sex, the bleak portrayal of a mental breakdown, and the heavily symbolic entries in Alex's journal that she refers to throughout. Nevertheless, it is of value in showing the agony of unresolved grief. Alex is still plagued by nightmares even after she is released from the hospital. She lives in constant fear of night, she frequently is unable to eat, and she cannot discuss Bradley even with her psychiatrist. Alex has other problems as well. Her mother's overprotectiveness, while understandable, hinders rather than helps. In addition, Alex has realized that her mother has always dominated the family and that Alex and her father have not ever been close. Slowly, however, she begins to resolve her difficulties, and the family relationships do change. Her father begins to be more assertive, frequently backing up Alex in front of the mother's often implacable wishes, and Alex does realize that her mother acts from love, not malice. Most importantly, she begins to discuss Bradley with the psychiatrist, realizing that she all along has felt sole guilt for his accident: "'Because if it hadn't been for me, if I hadn't come dragging along, he'd be alive . . . instead of dead'" (239). Finally, the tears come. The doctor helps her to understand that she has been running from her anger, her sadness, her guilt— "'You ran away for a long time, Alexandra, do you think you're ready to come back now?'" (250). Alex is beginning to heal: "I can say his name and the wound no longer bleeds. It's just a black-and-blue mark on my heart." When she accepts a date and returns to school, she knows that she will recover.

The major character in *Dance On My Grave* by Aidan Chambers experiences similar guilt. Three stumbling blocks result in a limited audience for this book: a rather large number of British expressions, a sophisticated style, and a major theme of homosexuality. Although the book has been classified as young adult reading, it is really an adult book. The perceptive, sensitive reader, however, can revel in its humor, its honesty, and its art. The book is rather avant-garde, composed of 117 "bits," several social worker's reports, two press clippings, some footnotes, and various other "fiascos." Hal is a bright, articulate, often self-effacing sixteen-year-old. His humor is marvelous, yet pathos reigns throughout as Hal tries to come to terms with the death of his friend and lover, Barry Gorman. From the beginning, as a result of a television show Hal saw as a child, Hal has been looking for a bosom friend. He thinks he has found his ideal in Barry, and both a friendship and a sexual relationship emerge, lasting only seven weeks. When Barry blatantly stays the night with a girl Hal has introduced him to, a terrible argument breaks out. When Barry attempts to follow Hal, who has run off, Barry is killed in a motorcycle accident. Further complications arise when Hal attempts to fulfill an oath he has made to Barry: to dance on Barry's grave.

Hal's reactions to the death of his friend are typical and numerous. Since Mrs. Gorman blames Barry's death on Hal, Hal is not able to seek her cooperation in letting him view the body. The girl over whom the two quarrel, Kari, devises a plan to get Hal into the morgue—he will dress as a woman and pose as Barry's grief-stricken fiancee. Although the scene is hilarious, the book does stress the need for one to see the dead body in order to accept the reality. Further, Hal experiences a myriad of reactions: numbness, guilt, sorrow, anger. Because he has not yet fulfilled his promise to dance on Barry's grave, he experiences severe migraine headaches which disable him for days. He also cannot erase the guilt—if the two hadn't quarreled, Barry would still be alive. He does come to realize, however, that he has been totally dependent upon Barry, that his very identity has been wrapped up in the older boy who has done all his thinking, all his planning. Likewise, he sees that Barry was not as ideal as he thought:

> It was your *idea* of Barry you wanted. Because the truth is that
> Barry wasn't what you thought he was.... Put on a rather good
> performance. As much for his own benefit as for yours. I think
> the truth is, Hal, that you fell for a face and a body and then
> put the person inside you wanted to find there (246).

Inherent in the book also are a number of other sensitive issues.
Hal begins to see his parents in a different light, having taken them
for granted and having been insensitive to their needs. (His father's
awkward but caring concern throughout Hal's ordeal is heartwarm-
ing.) Hal has also been going through the common struggle to
decide what he wants to do with his life, making difficult decisions
about future schooling and possible careers. By the end of the
novel, he has discovered much about friendship, revising his expectations to a more realistic level. He now can cope.

IV. The Death of a Relative

And you, my father, there on the sad height,
. . . .
Do not go gentle into that good night.
Rage, rage against the dying of the light.

"Do Not Go Gentle into That Good Night"
Dylan Thomas

The death of a pet is devastating; however, after a normal period of grief, life for the entire family goes on. Likewise, when a friend dies, even though the grief is longer and more difficult to overcome, eventually one finds new friends, renewed interests. The death of a relative, however, is a scary business. One can live without Fido, but how can one live without Daddy or Uncle Bill or Grandma or one's twin sister? The causes of death run the gamut from old age to suicide, from disease to automobile accidents, and ultimately reactions are the same—loss, fear, anger, guilt. But the immediacy of the death makes it more difficult to bear. Further, not only must the child reconcile his own grief, he must learn to understand and deal with the despair of the other family members. And each type of death—loss of an aunt or uncle, of a grandparent, of a sibling, of a parent—brings about its own special problems.

Perhaps the easiest of these is the death of a relative who is not of the immediate family. Books abound for younger children dealing with the death of an uncle or a grandparent; they follow a similar pattern, revealing basic truths. All establish the closeness between the relative and the child, show the agony following the death, and stress the beautiful memories of the loved one that will help sustain the child and enrich his life. Many include funeral rituals and also serve to calm a child's natural fears about his own death.

For instance, Linda Chandler's *Uncle Ike* begins by establishing the close relationship between Brent and his Uncle Ike, who lives in the apartment over the garage. The two spend a leisurely afternoon fishing and enjoying nature. The next day, however, Uncle Ike, working in the garden, asks Brent to bring him a drink of water. Brent returns to find his uncle collapsed. Although Brent efficiently calls an ambulance, Uncle Ike dies on the way to the hospital.

The next two days are filled with activities typical in a bereaved home. Friends bring food, and the family go to the funeral home. During the funeral, Brent remembers all that Uncle Ike has taught him: how to fish, how to catch a ball, how to be a good sport. The author explains briefly the ritual at the cemetery: the people gather, the minister says a prayer, and the family leaves. Brent is confused. He hopes fervently that Uncle Ike will be at home waiting for him. At home, disappointed, he sobs to himself and then restlessly wanders about the yard, finally forcing himself to enter Uncle Ike's apartment over the garage. Everything is the same, except that Uncle Ike is not there. Sobbing once again, Brent is joined by his father, who explains death to him: "'His body just gave out.... That happens to everyone. At some time in your life, there will be some reason why your body cannot continue to provide all you need'" (27). When Brent cries out that it's not fair for people to die, his father reminds him, "'... it is important for those of us who loved Uncle Ike ... to remember how kind he was'" (30) and reassures Brent that the feelings of grief will not last forever.

In Leone Anderson's *It's Okay To Cry*, a child, Ben, must help his younger brother, Jeremy, age five, accept the death of their Uncle Jeff, who was killed in a motorcycle accident. As they sit on the steps remembering all that they have done with their uncle, all that he has taught them, Jeremy does not yet realize that when someone has died, he will not return. Finally, Ben blurts out, "'Uncle Jeff died! ... he won't ... he won't be around anymore'" (18). Jeremy is immediately angry and defiant: "'Uncle Jeff is mean! Why did he have to die? He didn't want to teach me, that's why!... He could come back ... if he really wanted to'" (20–22). When Jeremy begins to cry, Ben imparts another lesson of Uncle Jeff's: It is okay to cry. Then he promises to teach Jeremy what Uncle Jeff has taught him.

Unfortunately, at the end of the book, the author has included a section called "Thinking and Talking," a didactic piece asking questions and giving interpretations of the story. While some of her suggestions would certainly be helpful to adults, their inclusion, covering funerals, the disposal of the body, and the reactions of the family, are heavy-handed.

Several books, all worthy, follow a similar pattern. In *Nana* by Lyn Littlefield Hoopes, *Nonna* by Jennifer Bartoli, *Why Did Grandpa Die?* by Barbara Shook Hazen, *When Grandpa Died* by Margaret Stevens, *My Grandpa Died Today* by Joan Fassler, and *Why Did Grandma Die?* by Trudy Madler, the grandparent has occupied a special part in the protagonist's life, usually surrounding activities: reading, swinging, gardening, taking walks. The grandparent falls ill and soon dies. Typical reactions follow: anger, inability to eat, tears. Most of these books explain the funeral, and some show the actual burial. In each case, the protagonist misses the grandparent, wishes for his return, but finally realizes the finality of death. And in each case, the book ends on a happy note. Left are happy memories and tangible reminders—a cookie recipe, pink lemonade, garden vegetables to harvest. In two of these books, before the death, the grandparent has explained mortality because he and his grandchild have come upon something dead, a bird in *When Grandpa Died* and a butterfly in *Why Did Grandpa Die?*, showing how an ailing person can help make his death easier to understand. Of the butterfly, Grandpa says, "'He's dead now. He doesn't breathe. . . . But it is nice to remember how he was when he was alive.'" Of the bird's death, Grandpa explains that all things die, that death is natural. "'Natural means that things turn out the way they are supposed to'" (10). He further explains that even after things die, they keep changing and that the bird's body will help flowers to grow.

All of the books do a decent job of explaining death in a simple, straightforward way. The best is probably *When Grandpa Died* because the accompanying photographs are both convincing and moving.

Charlotte Zolotow's *My Grandson Lew* points out the problem children have when their parents do not let them express their feelings or take part in the grief process. Lew, age six, awakes suddenly in the night and calls to his mother, complaining that he misses his grandfather. Lew's mother is amazed, since her father died when

Lew was only two. Nevertheless, Lew does have memories of his grandfather: his beard, his hugs, his comfort of Lew in the middle of the night, a trip to the art museum. Lew reveals that he has been waiting all these years for his grandfather to return, for although he lived far away, he always came back. Lew's mother realizes that she was mistaken in not telling Lew the truth. Then she begins to relate *her* memories of her father—his laughter, his pleasure in his grandson, his willingness to babysit. She tells Lew, "'But now we will remember him together and neither of us will be so lonely as we would be if we had to remember him alone.'"

Three books in this category deserve special consideration because of their ethnic insights. The title character of *Scat!* by Arnold Dobrin gets his name because he is constantly getting into things, disobeying, interrupting, and thus people tell him to "scat." Scat worships his father and wants to become a musician like him. Each night, his father plays a trumpet in a blues band, frequently taking Scat with him. Trouble arises when Scat's grandmother, the real boss of the family and a woman to be reckoned with, criticizes her son for playing jazz—"'Just wild, good-for-nothing noise! We're church-going people and we won't have any truck with that kind of low-down music'"—and insists that Scat not be allowed to accompany his father anymore.

Love of music seems inborn in Scat. Finally, his father gives him a harmonica for his birthday, an instrument Scat readily learns to play. Although Grandma does not like Scat's choice in music, she tells him to "'listen to what your heart says . . . not your head. You listen to what that little voice inside keeps saying. That'll set you straight. . . . The Bible says to follow the spirit—not the letter.'" Scat does not understand until one of the band members dies, and his father's band follows the casket to the cemetery, playing its music. Grandma, of course, is horrified because she finds this practice disrespectful. Later, when she herself dies, his father reassures Scat, "'Your grandma had a good long life. She had a lot of sadness but a lot of happy times too. . . . You know, I think she was tired. And kind of glad to be going!'" Scat realizes his father is right: "Grandma had a good life even if it was a hard one. But she had helped a lot of people and she sang and laughed and when she was tired—well, then, it was just time to say goodbye." Thus at her funeral, when Scat feels strange—"sad and happy, just the way a lot of jazz music sounded," he follows the spirit, not the letter, listens to his heart, not his head, and plays his harmonica as his last tribute to her.

In *The Happy Funeral* by Eve Bunting, the funeral of Laura's grandfather is a blend of both Chinese and American customs. Obviously Christian, the family still retain some Chinese customs. At the funeral home, for instance, each mourner gives a gift to accompany Grandfather to heaven. Laura draws a picture of the dog her grandfather had when he was a boy. Her mother tells her that the funeral will be happy, but Laura is confused. That night in bed, she is certainly not happy as she remembers the way he looked and the games they played. Laura cries herself to sleep.

The next day at the funeral, several pay tribute to their friend and loved one. When Laura looks at her grandmother and realizes that she, too, is old and will die soon, Laura is once again unhappy. Her mood later changes because of the coolness of the limousine, the jazzed-up tunes the marchers play. At the cemetery, however, everyone is crying. Laura suddenly understands her mother's words: "'When someone is very old and has lived a good life, he is happy to go'" (38) – but, Laura realizes, "she never said it was happy for us to have him go" (38).

Helen Coutant draws upon the Vietnamese culture in *First Snow*. Lien and her family are now living in New England and are eagerly awaiting the first snow. Used to almost tropical weather, Lien cannot imagine such a phenomenon. The child and her grandmother are particularly close, and they spend their afternoons poring over pictures of snow. One afternoon, when the first snowfall is predicted, the doctor tells the family that the grandmother is going to die. Uncertain of the meaning of the word, Lien seeks help from her grandmother, who tells her, "'Now listen carefully. If you go out into the garden and hold your hand up to heaven and are patient, you will have an answer to your question. You will discover for yourself what dying means.'" Although the day is bitterly cold, Lien perseveres until the snow begins to fall. She catches a snowflake on her finger, "a tiny, fleeing thing, beautiful and delicate." But it soon melts, rolls off her finger, falls to the ground and is gone. In dismay, Lien looks for it but instead discovers a tiny pine tree. Now she understands: "The drop of water had not really gone; it had only changed, like the snowflake, into something else," just as the tiny tree will change, just as her grandmother will change.

The book is powerful and moving. Opposed to the cold, to the oncoming death, are the beauty of nature, the growth of the pine tree, the loveliness of the white and yellow chrysanthemums in the pots on the windowsill in the cramped little closet that is the grandmother's room. Through the lyric prose of Coutant and through the wisdom of the grandmother, the reader feels the mystery and the beauty of life and of death.

A book deserving special merit because of its lyricism is Nancy Jewell's *Time for Uncle Joe*.

> It is spring again,
> and the lilac bush is fat and green
> and ready to bloom once more.
> Even the lilacs know
> It's time for Uncle Joe.

Year after year, Uncle Joe comes in the spring to visit until fall, assuming all the gardening chores and charming the first-person narrator, a girl, with his love and his humor. But Uncle Joe has died, leaving only memories.

At first, the child is desolate. She drags down from the attic the old cardboard box of his possessions and sleeps in his bed. Spring turns to summer, summer to fall, and the memories linger, particularly in nature. As the girl continues to pattern her behavior on the activities she shared with Joe in the past—lying in the hammock, slipping the dog pieces of food from the table—she begins to adjust; now she is able to put his things away. The next spring she realizes that Uncle Joe is never coming back, but as she smells the lilacs, Uncle Joe is still with her.

The most endearing work of all in this category is *Blackberries in the Dark* by Mavis Jukes. When Austin takes his yearly trip, he is not happy, for only his grandmother is there to meet him at the airport. His grandfather has died since Austin's last summer visit. When a neighbor offers to take him fishing, Austin declines, for he wants to fish only with Grandpa. Indeed, everything on the farm reminds him of his loss.

His grandmother is wonderful. She tries to interest him in re-stringing beads for an antique doll, part of her family for over a hundred years, but Austin does not know how to sew—or to fly fish, a skill his grandfather was to have taught him this summer. When they both end up in the barn, looking at Grandpa's fishing gear, they remember picking blackberries in the dark and eating the pie Grandma made in the middle of the night, and Grandpa's letting Austin wear his baseball cap and teaching him how to clean a trout. Finally, Austin's lethargy passes, and he agrees to pick blackberries for supper.

As he crawls down a steep bank near a creek and begins to pick the fruit, he hears ominous sounds from the surrounding woods. He is terrified, but then elated to find that the noise is coming from his grandmother, dressed in Grandpa's fishing clothes, complete with the baseball hat. The illustration is truly delightful. Together they figure out how to fly fish and decide simply to eat the blackberries as they are for supper. "'Good idea,' said his grandmother. 'Blackberries in the dark! It's a family tradition.'" Just as his grandfather would have done, they decide to throw the fish back for good luck. Later that night, Austin begins to string the beads for the doll, and Grandma presents him with his grandfather's fishing knife. Grandpa and family traditions will live on through Austin.

Older children, of course, may have even greater problems when a grandparent dies, since a deeper relationship may have developed and they are likely to be more sensitive towards the grief of other family members.

Books for children in the middle grades are less didactic, showing the grieving child not only coping with his loss but also dealing with other problems as well, thus giving additional insights into life. Further, most of these books have better literary style and better-developed characters. For instance, Elfie Donnelly's *So Long, Grandpa* has several stories in one. It offers, first of all, a portrait of a typical family. Michael Nidetzsky has quarrels with his sister Linda because she teases him and often picks on him; in turn, he is disgusted by her vanity and her preoccupation with her boyfriend. Michael also quarrels with his mother over homework, dirt, and his lack of punctuality. Nevertheless, the family is basically close. A second theme is that of maturation. Michael shares the typical concerns of a boy approaching puberty. He fears being thought a sissy; he worries what others think.

The main story deals with his grandfather's impending death. Although their relationship is not perfect (for instance, Michael is bored to death by Grandpa's tales of the war), they are close. His grandfather tells him special stories and seems to understand Michael's needs and desires. When Michael learns that his grandfather has cancer, the boy is not too concerned; he doesn't fully understand. At this point, his mother and father disagree, his mother wishing to hide from him reality, his father trying to include Michael in their discussions. The reader sees also what havoc is caused in a family when an elderly member is dying. During a trip to the Canary Islands, his mother lashes out: "'Suppose he dies out here? That'll make no end of trouble for us.'" Actually, she is simply letting her despair come out, but Grandpa's feelings are hurt, and he runs away. When Grandpa lashes out at her in return, he, too, is showing his anger over his condition.

Later on, Grandpa takes Michael to a funeral of an old crony and expresses his somewhat unconventional view on funerals, complaining of the vast amounts of money spent that will deprive the living of necessities, questioning why Christians cry when they should be "'singing and dancing for joy to think of a good Christian going to heaven'" (69).

The most effective part of the novel concerns the actual dying of Grandpa. Visible are the incredible pain he endures, the strain on the family, and the confused hurt of Michael when he cannot even see his grandfather. Michael feels that having attended one funeral, he is prepared for his grandfather's, but at the grave site he collapses. Actually ill, he goes to bed and can't seem to stop crying. His friend Ferdi helps by telling him not to feel sorry for himself, and when Michael reads the last words from Grandfather, a letter telling him to be happy and leaving to Michael all of his treasures, Michael realizes that his memories of his grandfather will sustain him.

Little Thunder, the protagonist of Craig Kee Strete's *When Grandfather Journeys into Winter*, gives more insight into death. Little Thunder and his grandfather, Tayhua, have a special relationship. The two often conspire against Little Thunder's mother, who, typically but kindly, keeps close reins on the two. Since Little

Thunder's father is dead, Tayhua becomes his mentor, guiding him, teaching him, loving him.

The book does give a rather bleak picture of life on an Indian reservation, and much social criticism is evident. For instance, Tayhua deplores the white man's values, principally centered around money and thus ignoring the beauties of nature. However, the book ceases to be didactic when the reader finds that although Tayhua deplores television openly, he nevertheless revels in the westerns he is addicted to—rooting for the Indians, of course.

When, at a round-up of sorts, a white man, Tanner, offers five hundred dollars for any man who can ride his wild and dangerous black stallion, Tayhua determines to ride the horse. At this point, Little Thunder learns that his grandfather is ill. His mother reveals that the doctors have restricted Tayhua's activities because of his heart. It has not occurred to Little Thunder to worry about his grandfather's age or his health. But Tayhua is adamant. When all the others fail to subdue the stallion, Tayhua insists that he be given a chance. Although Tanner is fearful for the old man (he certainly does not want anyone to be hurt), he—and Little Thunder's mother as well—realizes that it is a matter of pride for Tayhua to ride; further, Tayhua has asked that he be given the horse instead of money if he succeeds, for it has been his fondest wish to give his grandson a horse.

The ride is fierce and bloody. Although Tayhua eventually is able to subdue the horse and thus leave a legacy for his grandson, the ride proves too much for him. The exertion has caused great damage, and he realizes that death is near. The next day, Little Thunder is called home from school. On the way home, Little Thunder will not talk to the bus driver, who realizes the circumstances and is trying to show he cares. Little Thunder hugs his grief to himself, recalling all the beautiful memories he has of his grandfather—the jokes they have played on one another, the stories they have shared, the hunting and fishing expeditions. "Together they had shared a thousand things, large and small, and now inside himself Little Thunder knew those days of sharing were coming to an end" (62). When he gets home, friends and relatives are gathered outside the home, only to be sent away. Through his daughter-in-law, Tayhua thanks them for their love but expresses his need to be alone with his grand-son.

It is now time for Little Thunder to be "alone with him on the last day of his life on earth" (69). Little Thunder cries, and his grand-father gives to him his last gift, one last story describing life as a journey, like the life of a bird, through spring and summer into winter.

> "If the old birds never died, if they lived forever, there would be no place in this world for any new birds. My wings are weak with my old age. I am too tired to fly. A bird who cannot fly? No, it is not a good thing. But you are young. . . . Will you fly for me when I am gone?" (77-8).

Later, he insists that "'life must give way to life. It is the way of the world'" (81). Suddenly, they both hear the sound of wild geese, flying south for the winter. Helping his grandfather to the window, Little Thunder watches with him. Collapsing on the floor, Tayhua dies, but he leaves his grandson with an endearing philosophy: "We have . . . all been given a gift . . . given a gift of a journey . . . a journey into winter" (78).

Wisdom also comes to Sammy, the protagonist of *Family Secrets, Five Very Important Stories* by Susan Shreve. Because the book is seemingly a collection of short stories, it has no clear-cut ending. Nevertheless, it does read like a novel because it covers the family life of Sammy as he faces the realities, often painful, of grow-ing up. Among the problems he must face are the divorce of an aunt and uncle (adultery is involved) and the fear Sammy has that his mother and father may divorce. In another episode, Sammy, un-prepared for his math test, resorts to cheating. Even worse than cheating are the lies he tells his family; he has told his father his homework was done, and he lies that he has a stomachache because his guilt makes him hide in his room: "Now all of a sudden I've turned into this criminal. It's hard to believe I'm just a boy. And all because of one stupid math test" (52).

In both cases, his wonderfully warm and wise parents come through. Although they give him flippant answers when he asks if they are going to divorce—his father says not in the next two or three weeks and his mother replies that of course she was "getting a divorce—maybe even in the next fifteen minutes if Daddy was sitting in the living room reading the sports page. Which is just what he was doing" (14). Later they reassure him that they are not planning to divorce, but add, they can't promise that such an occurrence will never happen: "because certain things happen that you just don't plan for—but that it was very unlikely and they both loved me, which was first off what mattered and always would...." (23). Likewise, when Sammy admits to his father that he both lied and cheated, his father insists that he admit his crime to his teacher. Sammy says, "'Today I thought I was turning into a criminal.' Sometimes my father kisses me good night and sometimes he doesn't. I never know. But tonight he does" (58).

The same support comes through when Sammy deals with three other crises, all involving death. When he finds one of their dogs, Giles, dead, he can't even tell anyone. After school, he comes home, expecting a miracle. He hopes that Giles isn't dead any longer. He spends the afternoon in his room. "Mother told me later that sometimes when you have had a great sadness you need extra sleep" (11). The night after they bury Giles, Sammy kindly sleeps with his little brother Nicholas, who is grieving.

The family must also soon face the death of Sammy's grandmother, who has cancer. When Sammy's friend Amos is uncomfortable around Grandmama Welty because of the way she looks, Sammy realizes for the first time her palsy, her lack of teeth. And he realizes that she drinks far too much because of the pain. Although she is somewhat of a burden on the family, they all love her. Thus instead of going to Amos's house to play, Sammy returns to play gin rummy with Grandmama—"She beat me two times running" (46).

Finally, Sammy must face the suicide of Michael, the older brother of his best friend and neighbor Willy. As a result of the tragedy, the Henrys move, depriving Sammy of his best friend and leaving him sad and confused over the suicide. Sammy feels guilty because the only time he talked with Michael, he felt uncomfortable because Michael was six years older. He now feels that perhaps he could have helped, that Michael's death was his fault. Once again, his father comes through: "'It's nobody's fault.... We didn't know and the Henrys didn't know how lonely Michael was. Michael didn't tell anyone. If he had, someone would have been able to help him'" (33). Then he suggests that they call Willy and take him on a picnic. The love, support, and guidance Sammy receives emphasize the importance of family members during grief.

Unfortunately, Doris Orgel's *The Mulberry Music* minimizes this importance. Although Libby Feldman has less than perfect parents (doesn't everyone?), nothing indicates any reason for Libby's deep unhappiness or her overpowering love for her maternal grandmother. The grandmother, in turn, is almost too good to be true. She does have her eccentricities, but they simply emphasize her love of life and her independence; indeed, her unconventionality becomes a badge of honor. Equally unbelievable are the reactions of Libby to her grandmother's illness and eventual death. When Grandma first falls ill and is unable to take Libby swimming, Libby is devastated.

The book does give two valuable insights into death. The Feldmans, well-meaning, do more harm than good as they try to protect Libby. She is not allowed to see her grandmother, and they avoid discussing what the problem is. When Libby walks clear across town to visit her grandmother but finds no one home, she is truly devastated to find her grandmother is now in the hospital. She certainly should have been told. In addition, hospital rules that prevent anyone under twelve from visiting also produce trauma.

The book then lapses once again into unbelievable situations. Libby sneaks away again, goes to the hospital, and finds a doctor, coincidentally a friend of her grandmother's, who agrees to let Libby see her. Most children, particularly those as close to their grandmother as Libby is, would be glad, but Libby is sorry because of the changes in Grandma. This time she runs away to her grandmother's house, where the police find her and take her home.

Her parents don't do anything right about Grandma's illness but then surprisingly forgive Libby for running away three times, breaking into her grandmother's house, and causing general alarm. When Grandma dies, they let Libby make all the funeral plans—the funeral to be at Grandma's house with Libby's mother, an accomplished pianist, playing Grandma's favorite song. Most children could not identify with Libby or find any comfort in this book.

Falling loosely into the category of "death of a non-immediate relative" are two more books that include the death of an uncle. Of these, *Good-bye, Chicken Little* by Betsy Byars is not up to par for the author. Jimmie Little comes from a strange family. Indeed, most of the time, their behavior embarrasses him. As the novel begins, Jimmie's Uncle Pete, fortified with several beers, has bet some of his cronies that he can walk across the frozen river. When Jimmie arrives on the scene, he tries to talk to his uncle, who pays no attention. Inevitably, the ice cracks, and Uncle Pete disappears.

When Jimmie tells his mother what has happened, she lashes out at him: "'Why didn't you stop him? ... you should have stopped him!'" (20–1). Later, she apologizes, but "the talk with his mother in the living room had made him feel worse about Uncle Pete's death instead of better. There were some things you couldn't take back. They had already hit the mark, left a scar" (31). His guilt is compounded by his grief over his father's death in a coal mine. Then, when his best friend Conrad challenges him to stop moping, a fight ensues, ending with a black eye for Jimmie, broken Christmas gifts for Conrad, and an apparent end to their friendship.

Eventually, his crazy family helps. His older sister Cassie, usually preoccupied with her boyfriend, confesses that she, too, has felt enormous guilt because she had fought with their father the night before his death. Uncle C.C. helps as well. Leaving the nursing home to spend Christmas with Jimmie's family, Uncle C.C. bores them to tears, secretly yearns to return to the nursing home, but does help Jimmie—"'There's two parts to a man's life—up and down. . . . Your life goes up like a fly ball. . . . And then, like it or not, it starts down. And when it starts down, *you know it*'" (69). He adds, "'The people who are lucky have a long, long up and a quick down'" (70). His most precious bit of wisdom on life and death is that "people sat in the middle of life like babies in a room full of toys and whined to be amused," demanding *"meaning* when life is a *miracle"* (71).

Uncle C.C. is not the only guest that Christmas. Jimmie's mother has invited the entire family to a party, a festivity that turns into a tribute to Uncle Pete. The members laugh, dance, sing, and tell fond memories of Pete. Conrad, peeking in the window, is fascinated and asks to join in. Finally, the peace the family are offering begins to affect Jimmie. He can now go on with his life. Through the celebration of enjoying life and through the insight of Uncle C.C., Jimmie is able to resolve his grief.

The family in *Figgs and Phantoms* by Ellen Raskin makes

Jimmie's family seem dull indeed. While this book will have limited appeal, it is perfect for a select audience. First of all, many subtleties exist in the illustrations and the text, and the humor is sophisticated. In addition, a long dream sequence is heavily symbolic, and the themes are not blatant. Finally, as is usually the case with Raskin, the characters are bizarre. Nevertheless, anyone with a droll wit and a love of the grotesque will profit from the book and its many insights into both adolescence and death.

Mona, the protagonist, suffers from usual teenage complaints. She has pimples, she feels she is too tall, she is overweight as a result of eating to compensate for what she considers her many deficiencies. Most of all, she is ashamed of her family — understandably in her case, since they are not the usual sort of relatives. Her mother, Sis Figg Newton, not only teaches tap dancing but lives her entire life as a musical comedy, singing and dancing no matter what the occasion; her father, Newt Newton, is an unsuccessful used car salesman; other relatives include Auntie Grace Joe, the dog catcher; her husband, Kadota (and his nine performing "Kanines"); their son, Fido the Second; Uncle Truman, the Human Pretzel. No wonder that all the townspeople talk about the family and cause Mona even more humiliation. Mona's only salvation is Uncle Florence, a book dealer. When he dies, Mona wishes to die also.

Up to this point, Mona has rejected the family's peculiar religion, revolving around Capri. After Uncle Florence dies, Mona is unable to express her grief; instead, she plans to join him, looking for clues to the mysterious whereabouts of Capri. Falling ill, she has long, tortuous, heavily symbolic dreams. Out of these, she comes to terms with death, not only Uncle Florence's but her own. Probably his most precious legacy to her is the knowledge, wisdom and comfort that books can bring. Recalling bits and pieces of doggerel, poetry, and classical literature in her dream helps Mona understand.

Recovering from her illness, Mona awakes to find her family, still strange but always loving, joyfully welcoming her back to life. And the townspeople, too, respond. As she and three neighbors watch her family in the parade, Mona realizes that her family, for all its eccentricities, is loved and admired. She has a "lot of remembering to do, a lot of living and learning and loving to do" (152), before she returns to Capri.

Two more books also demand a sophisticated reader. In *Mollie Make-Believe* by Alice Bach, Mollie Fields lives in a totally ordered, almost neuter environment. Surrounded by wealth, family pressure, and rigid rules of conduct, she can never be herself. One finds no laughter, no freedom, no spontaneity. Although Mollie inwardly rebels, she, too, through conditioning, has adopted many of their ways—always keeping everything about her neat and orderly, feeling uncomfortable at any sign of sloppiness in others, always conscious of the image she must uphold. Most lacking in the family is any sign of outward warmth.

When her paternal grandmother falls ill, the same rigid behavior continues. None of the younger people even know what she is suffering from. Dutifully, they all—aunts, uncles and cousins—visit the apartment, carrying on as usual, keeping fresh flowers, ordering meals, and never, never mentioning illness or death. And crying is certainly not allowed. When her maternal grandparents died years earlier, and Mollie (of course not allowed to attend the funeral) asked about it, her dad said, "'Mollie, it's not the sort of thing you discuss. It is very sad, and we shall all miss Gram and Grampa very much. But life goes on'" (49). One wishes for one sign of humanness but is consistently disappointed. When the doctor arrives each day, all the men rush to put on their suit coats. Propriety reigns.

Mollie has mixed emotions about her cousin Holly. Even though Mollie tries to be everything the family demands, Holly always seems to be the favorite even though she breaks the rules constantly. Thus Mollie resents Holly, envies her, and admires her. Mollie also has difficulty with boys. She has been dating David, who is "comfortable," who meets her family's expectations, whom she doesn't have to think about. Then one day, taking a walk in a brief respite from the vigil at her grandmother's, she meets Jamie, a boy who lives freely and unconventionally. For days, he is the focal point of her life, but when he attempts to seduce her, she flees in panic.

Many of Mollie's conflicts her Aunt Pat helps to resolve.

> "When you are living by your own rules, you don't have to ask anybody—and you are an adult.... We all share our rules with you so that you will know how we think life should be lived. But

when you are an adult you will be making your own decisions about how you live. And there will be no reason to hide anything, because you won't be breaking anybody's rules but your own. And you can't keep secrets from yourself" (138).

Unfortunately, Mollie is still unable to express her emotions. If nothing else, the book is an excellent manual on how *not* to handle grief.

Admittedly, *A Ring Of Endless Light* by Madeleine L'Engle is splendidly written, with well-developed characters and intrinsic interest for the older reader, particularly female, because of the many romantic triangles involved. Admittedly, too, the book required much thoughtful research and contains many perceptive ideas. Its major drawback is that death permeates it from beginning to end.

The novel starts at a funeral. Vicki Austin is attending the funeral of a dear friend of her family's, Commander Rodney. He has suffered a fatal heart attack after rescuing a would-be suicide from the ocean. Vicki knows the would-be suicide, Zachary, and soon becomes deeply involved with him. She wants to help him, even though his impulsive and dangerous streak frightens her and he is far more advanced sexually than she.

In the meantime, Vicki and her family must also face the impending death of her grandfather, who has leukemia. Zachary's mother, too, has died in the previous year, perhaps triggering his suicide attempt. Another young man, Adam, who eventually captures Vicki's heart, has faced the death of a good friend because a girl Adam was involved with was actually a spy after scientific research. As a result of Adam's blind love for her, he trusted her; now he feels guilty over his friend's death. Adam's boss, Jeb, has also lost his wife and child the previous year in a tragic automobile accident. Later in the book, a motorcyclist hits Jeb, and he lies close to death. Near the end of the book, Vicki becomes acquainted with a small child, Binney, at the hospital. Eventually, Binney dies in Vicki's arms. And throughout, we are aware of the atrocities around the world—mass murderers and fishermen killing hordes of dolphins. The family is even worried about a family of swallows nesting above their front door; because the nest is so shallow, they fear the birds will fall to their death.

Interwoven among all of these gruesome events are numerous discussions among the various characters that touch upon many aspects of death: cryonics (a process by which a dead body is frozen in hopes that in the future we may have the knowledge to revive the person); the traditional view of heaven; the morality of keeping people on life-support systems; the ethics involved in withholding medical care for religious reasons. In additon, several of the characters give their own particular views on death. These conversations are a bit hard to swallow (normal, everyday people are not usually that articulate or philosophical), and Vicki, not yet sixteen, is unusually perceptive for a girl her age.

Nevertheless, the book will give the more mature reader much to ponder, and it does, in the end, offer affirmation. Adam, in his scientific work with dolphins, enlists Vicki's aid. She has a peculiar knack of communicating with these animals. Not only do they offer fascination, but they are able to take her mind off her troubles, and when she seems unable to recover from the many shocks of the summer, it is the dolphins who comfort her and bring her back to the magical world of the living.

More difficult than the death of an uncle, an aunt, a grandfather, or a grandmother is the death of a sibling. Siblings fight; they often wish the other were dead; they frequently are jealous of one another. In any case, guilt is a natural reaction; sometimes a child may even feel responsible for his sibling's death. But the child does not live in a vacuum. His parents may cause more problems. They may cling to the surviving child, putting undue pressure on him to "replace" the lost child. In other cases, the parents may withdraw into their own grief, depriving the surviving child of the necessary love, comfort, and understanding he needs.

Gloria H. McLendon is well qualified as a teacher, a writer, and a lecturer on the effects of grief on children. Her book *My Brother Joey Died* is almost a textbook on the loss of a sibling. When her brother Joey dies, the main character, a girl of around ten, feels guilt, not only because she has on occasion wished him dead, but because he has died of the virus he caught from her. Although her grandparents are sympathetic, her friends reject her, and her parents withdraw, frequently criticizing her and fighting with each other. She finally believes that her parents don't love her. When she begins acting up in school, a counselor suggests a support group.

Later, her parents, too, seek professional help so that the family does come together again in an attempt to get on with life. Unfortunately, the author does not show her readers, but tells them. The main character does not even have a name; the reader does not see any other part of her character or her life; and the dialogue during the support group sessions is stilted and unreal (the counselor talks like a programmed computer). Other books in this genre are much more effective in their style, their insights, their development of character.

For instance, two books for younger children, both with marvelous illustrations, tastefully introduce the subject of a sibling's death. The primary function of Joanne Oppenheim's *James Will Never Die* is to capture the wonderful imagination and creativity of children. Tony, his brother James, and their friends Bobby and Kenny have wonderful adventures through fantasy: They are pioneers crossing the Rocky Mountains; they go on an archeological dig; they are aliens from outer space; they climb Mount Everest (the illustrations show the power of their imagination; for instance, the top of the tool shed becomes a precipice of sheer ice as the snow whirls around). Two problems exist, however, for Tony. James, the older brother, always captures the juiciest roles, and no matter what, he never dies—"'How come James can live through an avalanche, enemy fire, and everything else?'" Finally, Tony hits upon an infallible scheme. He suggests that they play pirates, knowing full well that James will insist upon being the captain. When a storm hits, the captain, of course, must go down with his ship.

In the life boat, the three friends toss on the open sea—"Our pirate ship was gone and so was James." Suddenly, Tony starts to feel bad about James. When he spots his brother floating on a piece of the mast, he leaps into the sea to save him: "I could have let him drown or let the shark finish him off ... but I didn't. I saved him, and I wasn't sorry. It was worth it to hear him say, 'Tony, I owe you my life.'"

Many children will identify with Tony, who seldom wins out over his older, more clever sibling. They will also identify with his hidden desire for a sibling to die. At the end, however, Tony realizes how much he truly cares for James and sees that he, too, can hold his own.

Nadia, a Bedouin, the daughter of the sheik Tarik, legitimately gets her name, *Nadia the Willful*, the title of a story by Sue Alexander. Only her older brother Hamed can tease her out of her moods, calm her temper. When Hamed rides out on his own and is killed by the drifting sands of the desert, everyone is inconsolable. Particularly affected are Nadia and Tarik. After a week, Tarik makes a pronouncement: "'From this day forward . . . let no one utter Hamed's name. Punishment shall be swift for those who would remind me of what I have lost.'"

Everyone suffers from this edict but dares not disobey. Nadia obeys with difficulty, for everything she sees and does reminds her of her brother – the tales he told her, the black lamb that he loved. Eventually, her despair increases her willfulness so that everyone flees at her approach. Finally, she can no longer stand the pain. She begins to speak of Hamed to others, teaching them what he has taught her, repeating his tales. As she remembers, so do the others, and for all, the hurt lessens.

Unfortunately, one day a shepherd, thinking he is talking to Nadia, speaks Hamed's name – to Tarik, and is immediately banished from the oasis. In fear, the others refuse to listen to Nadia talk of her brother. "And the less she was listened to, the less she was able to recall Hamed's face and voice. And the less she recalled, the more her temper raged within her, destroying the peace she had found." In desperation, she goes to her father. He admits that he can no longer remember Hamed's face or his voice. She shows him the way: In remembering Hamed, "'There is a way that Hamed can be with us still.' . . . And Hamed lived again – in the hearts of all who remembered him."

Most of the books for older children concentrate on specific difficulties, and likewise, most avoid pat endings. Four of these deal with the death of a twin. In two, we see the unique relationship twins share; they enjoy a closer identification, but also must struggle to keep their individualism.

Chas Carner's *Tawny* suffers from sentimentality in parts and from an exaggerated plotline, but is still worthwhile. Part I deals with the tragedy of the Landry family. Hunters, poaching on the Landry farm, have accidentally shot and killed Trey's twin brother, Troy. While the accident is plausible, the aftermath isn't. We do see the grief of all the family members, but never once do we hear of the attempts by law officials to find the killer, a matter that would have preoccupied the family and lacking resolution, would have tormented them.

Through flashbacks, Trey remembers his brother with love and with awe, for Troy was the brave one, always in trouble, always experimenting, fearlessly pursuing life. And Trey is uncomfortable on Mother's Day when he realizes that he must be the one to compensate for his parents' loss. Otherwise, the subject of death gets short shrift. The book rather centers around the hard work on the farm and several disasters, including a barn fire, more menacing hunters, and a devastating storm.

The most important compensation Trey finds is the title character of the book. Again, hunters have wreaked havoc, seriously wounding a doe that the Landrys take to their farm and nurse back to health. Tawny becomes Trey's friend, his pet. Time and time again, Tawny's existence is threatened. The biggest conflict, however, surrounds the necessity to retrain the doe to live in the wilds again. Trey painstakingly teaches the deer, but resists letting go of her. His mother assures him, "'When someone truly loves another, he can't feel possessive, because that is a one-sided love that hurts the other'" (139). Just when Trey has made up his mind to let Tawny go, she disappears, and he is in despair, experiencing nightmares. A month later, however, Tawny returns, accompanied by a buck. Trey runs to her, removes her pet collar, tells her he loves her, and lets her go forever.

Inge, too, in My Twin Sister Erika by Ilse-Margret Vogel, suffers in comparison with her twin; she is definitely less assertive than Erika. In their "courting" of the older and thus glamorous neighbor Magda, Erika always wins. To court the favor of them both, Inge sacrifices and is overly generous. As a result, she is often abused. For instance, when she agrees to give up her new doll so that Magda will return Erika's, Magda returns the doll, after a long week, with its beautiful long blonde hair cut. Both twins see Magda for what she is, however, when they spend hours and hours building a house outdoors and Magda is less than impressed and treats them rudely.

Most importantly, Inge is not certain who she is because of her close identification with Erika. And the game they play, switching the red and blue hair ribbons that help outsiders to identify them, increases her confusion. She wants to be herself and thus resents

Erika's power over her, yet sometimes they share a special harmony. "It was wonderful to have a sister. A twin sister to share butterflies with, and running brooks and leaping squirrels, and birds and blades of grass and wild flowers. It felt so good to feel as one" (41).

Then suddenly Erika falls sick and dies. At first, Inge feels not lonely but important—she is ". . . 'the only one now, the only one'" (44). Later, however, when she sneaks in to look at Erika's body, she is not sure who has died. She continues to enjoy the novelty of being all alone, of having exclusive rights to Magda, of owning all the toys. Suddenly, she realizes how much she misses Erika. And she reveals that one time she had wished Erika dead. But her mother reminds her that Erika had wished Inge dead too, and that neither one of them really was serious. Inge's real awakening occurs when she realizes that her mother misses Erika more than Inge does and vows to give her mother enough love for two. "Now I'm helping her, I thought, and I was happy" (54).

While Trey and Inge struggle to find their own identity in the absence of their twins, Jenny McGregor, in *Home From Far* by Jean Little, feels incomplete without her twin brother, Michael, who has been killed in an automobile accident. Months later, she has still not adjusted. To complicate matters, her parents decide to take in as foster children a boy Jenny's age, coincidentally named Michael as well, and his younger sister, Hilda. During the rest of the book Jenny must adjust to both changes in her life.

At first, Jenny is deeply resentful of both children, particularly Michael, for he seems to be taking the place of her twin. The dog immediately takes to him, the other children accept him, and he takes over many of her brother's possessions—his room, his tennis racket, his place in the affections of her parents. Compounding the problem is Jenny's fear that her mother is not really grieving for Michael, that Jenny is the only one who truly cares. Later, she realizes how wrong she has been. She and her mother discuss the situation, and her mother admits that wrongly she has been trying to spare the children, not wishing them to suffer as *she* has in the past from letting "'memories grow to be the burden. . . . I imagined you sitting brooding over the accident and cherishing Michael's things as though they were more important than Michael himself'" (123).

Jenny and the new Michael do grow close, initially because they gang up on Alex, Jenny's nine-year-old brother, who has become a sneak and a tattletale. Later, Jenny realizes Alex's problem. After her twin dies, she feels odd-man-out. She and her twin had always been a team, just as Alex and the youngest child, Mac, were a team. Now, she has her new foster brother, Mac has Hilda, and Alex has no one.

A final problem concerns the foster children. While their mother is dead, they do have a father who simply isn't able to care for them properly. Michael is torn: He is beginning to love his foster family and to feel a part of them, yet he does not want to be disloyal to his own father, Pop. When Pop offers to give him a home, however humble, they both agree that Mike belongs with the McGregors.

The family in *Laura's Gift* by Dee Jacobs are also reticent about discussing matters of illness and death. Laura and Catherine are twins, but certainly not identical. While Laura is quiet, responsible, and insightful, Catherine is flippant, outspoken and careless. The biggest difference, however, is that while Catherine is a healthy child, Laura has a form of muscular dystrophy and is confined to a wheelchair. Catherine has accepted Laura's handicap, but she has not come to terms with the true nature of the illness. When she reads about the disease at the public library, she realizes that Laura is soon to die. Almost immediately, they both contract the flu. Laura must be hospitalized, and when she develops pneumonia, Catherine is desperate. Unfortunately, her parents have not discussed the illness with Catherine at Laura's bidding. Thus Catherine misinterprets their behavior. For instance, she is furious when they redecorate the room she and Laura share; she feels that they are already wiping out any reminder of Laura.

Catherine falls behind in her studies and decides to drop her beloved piano lessons. Strangely enough, it is Miss Vertue, the teacher she has always considered an enemy, who is finally able to communicate with her. Miss Vertue is willing to discuss the possibility of Laura's death.

"And sometimes it helps to talk about our fears and to know that others have them too ... to know we're not alone" (48).

She then tells Catherine Laura's gift to her: "'Laura has enough discipline for the two of you; she sees to it you stay on course'" (48). And she explains Catherine's gift to Laura: "'You give to her your sense of fun, a necessary ingredient in everyone's life, but especially for her'" (48).

Now Catherine is able to discuss openly the possibility of Laura's death. When her younger brother Jeff, up to this point simply an annoyance, expresses *his* fears, Catherine is able to comfort him. When their parents are called to the hospital and everyone fears that this is Laura's last night, Jeff and Catherine put together a model—"'Because at a time like this, Cath, building a blimp is absolutely the safest thing to do'" (52).

Happily, Laura does show signs of recovery once more. And Catherine is able to discuss her feelings with her parents. Laura has begun to accept her fate, and they admit that they were wrong not to have discussed the matter before.

Again, in Mary Stolz's *By the Highway Home,* because of the inability of the family members to discuss their loss, their grief continues. Catty, thirteen, is miserable. Her older sister is a constant problem. And normal sibling rivalry is not the issue here, for Ginger is not a likeable person; she cannot keep friends, even boyfriends, although she is bright and beautiful, and her parents, the Reeds, know that she is vain, self-absorbed, and often cruel. In addition, Mr. Reed has lost his job, and the family must move from Indianapolis to Vermont to help a great-uncle run an inn for elderly people. Most of all, Catty is still suffering over the loss of her brother, Beau, who has been killed in Viet Nam.

Several significant themes appear in the book. Catty continues to wish that she and her sister could have the sort of relationship that Catty has read about. Time after time, however, Ginger rejects any offer Catty makes to put their relationship on a happier basis. References to the future throughout the book indicate that the two will never be close. In discussing Beau's death, the author has provided provocative material dealing with pacifism and the ugliness of war. As always in Stolz's books, a warm regard and respect for nature emerge. And an insight into old age also appears: the need for the old to be necessary, and the inevitable withdrawal from life that the elderly must face.

Most important, however, is the treatment of death. Catty's

grief has been prolonged to an unnecessary degree simply because none of the other family members are able to talk about Beau. Although Catty wants to talk about him, any mention brings despair to her family and then guilt to Catty.

> "I guess Mom and Daddy can't except I think I loved him as much as they did and I want to. Ginger just looks over my head and waits for me to finish if I start saying anything. And Lex is too young, really. He has this way of—of not seeming to know that Beau is dead" (124).

Finally, Catty is able to talk about her brother to others outside the family, and all of them—even Ginger—become more content with their lives, taking an active joy in their work and in nature. But the major problem is not resolved for any of them.

Another book that ends on a less than happy note is *Beat the Turtle Drum* by Constance C. Greene. The major part concentrates on the particularly warm and loving relationships among thirteen-year-old Kate, eleven-year-old Joss, and their parents, so that we feel the full impact of grief when Joss falls from a tree and dies instantly from a broken neck. Kate, who narrates the story, is a precocious but loving child. Planning to be a writer, she uses ostentatious vocabulary, but does show true creativity; for instance, she determines that all people have distinctive smells (her sister smells like "a puppy that has just had a bath" and "chewing gum that has been chewed awhile" [42]). Likewise, her sensitivity allows her to make adult-like judgments on those around her; it also makes her a perceptive narrator.

Joss, of course, is also central to the novel. After her death, one woman says of her, "'She was so gay, so, I don't know, so clean, if you know what I mean. So alive'" (107). Perhaps the best indication of Joss's character is her relationship with Hootie, a chubby eight-year-old who is not bright and suffers difficulty with his family, who are all super-achievers. Joss befriends him, encourages him, and protects him.

Kate suffers the normal reactions to the death of a sibling. She feels guilty that Joss died, not she, and she feels resentful of her mother's dependence on her—"'Just be here,' she said. 'Don't go away. I want to know where you are, Kate. You're all I have left'"

(98). At first, she doesn't want to go to the funeral; but later, she is glad that she does, because she can see Joss for one last time. Her cousin Mona helps Kate by explaining the way brothers and sisters feel:

> "They feel guilty, because they fought or were jealous of lots of things. And here they are, alive, and the other one is dead. And there's nothing they can do. It'll take time, Kate." (105–6).

Mrs. Mahoney, the children's third-grade teacher, also comforts Kate in a letter, telling her that Kate will always take pleasure in memories of Joss, in telling her own children about her beloved sister, in perhaps even naming one of her children after Joss.

Unlike many books, however, *Beat the Turtle Drum* ends while the family is still in the midst of grief. Kate's mother is still relying on tranquilizers and sleeping pills, her father on bourbon and scotch, and Kate herself still grieves silently. She knows that in time the hurt will fade, but says, in her final words, "It's the right now that hurts" (119).

Two books concentrate on the guilt a sibling may suffer. In a few brief pages of *Nobody's Fault*, Patricia Hermes brilliantly captures the familiar relationship between Emily, probably around eleven or twelve, and her thirteen-year-old brother, Matt, whom she calls Monse, short for "Monster." One minute Monse is making fun of Emily; the next he is helping her perfect her catching skills and letting her wear his treasured baseball cap. Told from Emily's somewhat naive point of view, the story shows her conflicts: Her best friend is growing up and is thus losing interest in baseball; Emily herself is afraid of the ball; and she is unable to see any of her own culpability in the fights she has with Monse.

Then a tragic accident occurs. While cutting the grass, Monse is attacked by sand wasps, and in his attempt to get away, he jumps or falls off the lawn mower. The mower runs over him, and he bleeds to death. While many of the normal responses to grief appear, the main emphasis is on guilt. Emily tries to pretend that Monse is not dead, that he is in the hospital but will return. Her denial is typical but has additional dimensions: If she is to admit he is dead, she must also admit that she is to blame. For when the accident occurred, Emily was in Monse's bedroom, out of earshot, putting a dead snake in his bed in retaliation for one of his tricks. Thus she refuses to leave her room, sleeping hour after hour, for in sleep, she can disassociate herself.

Her parents, loving, warm, and sensible, recognize that Emily's reaction is abnormal and thus seek the help of a psychiatrist. Through Emily's repeated visits with Dr. Weintraub, she is able to admit her shameful secret that she was "responsible" for Monse's death, only to learn that everyone involved feels guilt: her mother for not waiting for the housekeeper to arrive; the housekeeper for having had her hair done; her father for having told Matt to cut the grass before ball practice. Emily cries out, "'It's nobody's fault! Accidents happen.'"

Now that she has purged herself of responsibility, Emily can go through the normal grief process. She is able to cry, to visit his grave, to recall how much she loved him, to remember their last special moment together. As she leaves the grave with Matt's baseball cap in place, she remembers his smile, "his real smile, not his teasing one," and his last words to her, "'Keep your body in front of the ball.'" She is ready to begin life again.

Beyond Silence by Eleanor Cameron has three plots intertwined. Andrew Cames and his father are visiting their ancestral castle in Scotland. On the plane ride, Andrew begins to have vivid visions, a type of precognition, revolving around a girl named Deidre. Upon reaching the castle, he is given a letter written a hundred years before but never mailed; it is addressed to Andrew Durrel Cames, obviously an ancestor. The contents of the letter open up many other occurrences in which Andy hears Deidre's voice, sees her playing as a child, is led by her away from a group of cattle. The explanations of these occurrences are full of jargon and difficult to believe.

In the meantime, Andy is having a silent war with a guest at the castle, the Quark, a lonely but pushy man whom Andy instantly dislikes. Because the Quark is getting his Ph.D. in philosophy and somehow realizes that Alex is experiencing unusual psychic phenomena, Andy is determined to hide from him, to rebuff him.

Finally, the reader learns that Andy and his family are still trying to recover from the death of Andy's older brother Hoagy. Hoagy served in Viet Nam, was wounded, and was on heavy medication for pain, which was likely responsible for the car crash that killed him. Andy's mother blames her husband for not trying to prevent Hoagy from enlisitng. The two have an uneasy truce, and she has immersed herself in her writing, refusing even to accompany them on the trip. We learn that eventually the two divorce, not an uncommon result of a death of a child.

After intricate investigations by Andy concerning his ancestor and the mysterious Deidre and elaborate plotting to thwart the Quark and his curiosity, Andy finally realizes the source of his recurring nightmares: He, too, feels guilt for the death of his brother. On the night of the accident, Hoagy had asked Andy to drive, but Andy, only fifteen, an inexperienced driver, refused to drive down the narrow mountain road and instead rode with Hoagy's girlfriend. The reader assumes that once Andy has made this realization, he can begin to recover from his loss.

The biggest problem is that only a fragile connection exists between Andy's precognition and his guilt. In one vision, when Deidre mentions her own guilt, he suddenly realizes his. And the animosity against the Quark, who one day disappears after the death of a professor he wholly admired, is never fully believable. Indeed, most of the characters in the book, while recognizing his less desirable traits, nevertheless feel sorry for the man on the one hand and admire his intelligence on the other. Perhaps the most positive insight offered is Andy's reclaiming his heritage. He plans to return to Scotland the following summer and to attend college there. Perhaps in this way, he can keep the memory of his brother alive.

Finally, *Uncle Mike's Boy* by Jerome Brooks shows a family nearly destroyed by the death of a child. Virgil Lewen, known as Pudge, is one tough little eleven-year-old. He has to be. In a brutally frank manner, the book opens with Pudge and his little sister Sharon clinging together at the top of the stairs as their divorced parents fight. Like many siblings in this situation, the two are close as they give each other comfort; Pudge and Sharon have even begun an organization called SAFE—Society Against Family Excitement. Pudge has other problems as well. He worries constantly about his weight, he lives in constant fear of three neighborhood bullies, and he yearns to have a relationship with a schoolmate, Dina.

Suddenly all these problems are compounded when Sharon is killed in a freak accident. Not only does Pudge feel responsible, the loss sends his father deeper into alcoholism and depression; Mr. Lewen eventually ends up in a mental hospital. Meanwhile, Mrs. Lewen continues to seek refuge with her psychiatrist, failing to give to Pudge the comfort and understanding he seeks.

Throughout, it is evident that Pudge worships his father, secretly wishing to live with him, vowing to be a poet in his father's footsteps. Luckily, he finds a perfect substitute in his Uncle Mike. The title of the novel suggests what Pudge finally comes to realize: He *is* Uncle Mike's boy. He looks like him, they understand each other and are able to communicate, and Uncle Mike gives him the experiences he needs: they go fishing, Pudge works part-time in Uncle Mike's shoe store, and they are able to discuss all of Pudge's problems.

Another source of comfort comes from Pete Rossiter, the son of the school gym teacher. An eighth-grader wise beyond his years, Pete accepts Pudge for what he is, encourages him, and shows him that one can overcome family problems. When Pudge's mother later decides to marry Pete's father, the reader assumes that they will be excellent stepbrothers.

Pudge's relationship with Dina likewise evolves. While he is attracted to her as a girl, she also becomes a true friend. Pudge even manages to deal with the school bullies and with his teacher, who often treats him unfairly. Specifically, after she has punished him for something he didn't do, she rescinds the punishment for the wrong reason—because he has lost his sister.

Although Pudge faces incredible conflicts, his biggest is, of course, the loss of Sharon. After he realizes that he was not responsible for her death, he goes through a long period of mourning, never forgetting her, trying to be courageous for her sake. He will survive, his mother is getting on with her life, but Mr. Lewen falls victim to the loss. As Pudge says, "'I don't think Dad'll ever read my poems'" (221).

In contrast is Robert Burch's *Simon and the Game of Chance*, wherein death actually strengthens the family. Simon dislikes his father, Mr. Bradley. This conflict is not a result of typical rebellion from a maturing boy, for all his brothers respond in much the same way. Only Clarissa, the oldest child and the only girl, occasionally defends her father. Mr. Bradley suffers from a fundamentalist religion that demands instant obedience, discourages any type of frivolity, and allows little room for humor or for fun.

When Mrs. Bradley delivers a baby girl, the family rejoice but worry because the infant is weak and ill, requiring further hospitalization, and because Mrs. Bradley has experienced emotional difficulties in the past. When the baby dies, Mrs. Bradley has a nervous breakdown and requires hospitalization.

The bulk of the novel centers around the children's struggle to keep the house running while anticipating the wrath of their father without their mother's calming influence. Little by little, Mr. Bradley begins to loosen up, but Simon faces another problem. Clarissa, whom he adores, has fallen in love with Whit Stovall. When they announce that they will marry, Simon is devastated. He even wishes that something will happen to prevent the marriage. Tragically, the day of the wedding, the furnace in the barbershop explodes, killing Whit, who is waiting to get his hair cut. Simon must suffer not only the despair of his sister but also the guilt he feels.

The treatment of Clarissa's grief is totally believable. She becomes quiet and withdrawn, seeking the solace of her room most of the time. Finally, after a month has passed, she begins to take part in the family again at the insistence of their father, who suggests that the boys do less for her, not more. Keeping busy and being responsible are the therapy she needs. Once again, however, disaster threatens Simon, for now she plans to go away to school. And once again, Simon selfishly hopes that something will intervene. He soon realizes, however, that he is being selfish. In a long talk with his father, he admits that he has tried to sabotage her plans and in the process learns a great deal about his father – a man who had too many responsibilities as a child, living in poverty with an alcoholic father. Simon realizes that the things that happened to his father had "helped turn him into the man he'd become. . . . He no longer hated his father, and maybe that was enough for now" (116). When Mrs. Bradley finally returns home, the future looks optimistic, and Simon is on his way to maturity.

When a child dies, family support becomes ultimately crucial. Virginia Lee in *The Magic Moth* immediately establishes the warmth and closeness of the Foss family. Maryanne, age ten, a victim of a heart defect who is soon to die, cannot join the ritual birthdays the family celebrates each time the mother bakes a cake, honoring not only the family members but also the pets.

Although Maryanne is bedridden and the children are totally aware of her illness, they are still not prepared when their father tells them that she "'will have to go away soon'" (12). Particularly distraught is Mark-O, age six. He does not understand why Maryanne sleeps all the time and why she will barely talk to him. In the meantime, normal family activity continues. Maryanne lies in her bed waiting for a cocoon she has saved to hatch; Barbara, age fourteen, is assuming more adult duties around the house; Stephen, fifteen, stays in his own world; Julie, age nine, is still always late; and Mark-O gains a new interest, planting grapefruit seeds.

When Maryanne worsens and the doctor explains that she will not last through the night, the parents wisely let the children stay up to say their last good-byes to her. As Maryanne dies, a moth emerges from the cocoon and flies out the window.

Following are typical preparations and typical reactions. Julie and Mark-O, because of their age, express confusion. Their mother has explained that Maryanne "'will go to sleep and not know she is here. The important part of her, that does the dreaming, will be someplace else'" (26). Likewise, the minister tells the children, "' . . . when people die they step through a door into another place that we can't see with our eyes'" (45). When asked if he is speaking the truth, he simply says, "'That is what I believe'" (45). Confusion also results for Mark-O because of the many visitors and the funeral itself (strangely enough, none of the family ever view the body). Tears abound, of course, but Mark-O has not yet resolved his grief.

Two sources eventually give comfort. As one of the grapefruit seeds sprouts, the children resolve to plant it and name it the Maryanne Tree. And Mark-O is inspired to draw a picture of the moth. Although they are not yet able to sing, all are beginning to look forward again.

The most affirmative yet realistic book is *A Summer to Die* by Lois Lowry. Molly, fifteen, and Meg, thirteen, do not get along. Molly is beautiful, neat, tactful, and sure about her future (she will marry and have six children). Meg is awkward, impulsive, and unsure both about the present and the future. Gradually they are beginning to resolve their differences when Molly becomes ill. Eventually she is to die of leukemia.

The author gives us a clear picture of what illness can do both to the victim and to the family around. Because Molly has always been obsessed with her looks, the loss of her hair, her weight loss, her listlessness, combined with her physical discomfort, turn her usually sunny disposition into grouchiness. Later, she really withdraws from the family, seemingly content with her new interest in wildflowers. For the others, life is also difficult. While they do go on with their lives as best they can, the shadow of her illness and later of her impending death causes tension and misery.

After Molly's death, the author does not dwell, as so many do, on the immediate effects on the family. The reader sees nothing of the funeral or the individual reactions of the family.

> Time goes on, and your life is still there, and you have to live it. After a while you remember the good things more often than the bad. Then, gradually, the empty silent parts of you fill up with sounds of talking and laughter again, and the jagged edges of sadness are softened by memories.
>
> Nothing will be the same, ever, without Molly. But there's a whole world waiting, still, and there are good things in it.

The most beautiful aspect of this book, the quality that makes it a valuable work on death even though it ignores many of the psychological and practical matters concerned with the loss of a family member, is its emphasis on the quality of life available to us.

Because the family is educated (the father is a university professor on leave to write a book), their interests are varied. Meg's avocation (the reader suspects it will be her vocation as well) is photography. Lowry is able to capture, through descriptive detail and imagery, the marvelous beauty of the photographs Meg takes. Beauty is available for Molly, too, through her fascination with wildflowers. Both of these interests receive reinforcement through their neighbor, Will Banks, an elderly man who retains a lively interest in the world and represents the second prerequisite to a full life—friendship. The two girls also befriend Ben and Maria, a young couple who bother the rural community because of their nonestablishment activities and beliefs: Although they are married (a point some villagers question), Maria keeps her maiden name; they grow organic vegetables and refinish furniture; Maria is to have her baby at home. Molly and Meg learn much from these totally alive people, and the expected baby gives Molly an additional interest.

Equally important are the love and the humor that permeate the Chalmers' household. Knowing each other well, understanding and accepting, even cherishing the idiosyncracies that make each unique, they flourish.

Even though Molly has died, her brief life makes the reader feel happy and content, and he knows that Meg, with her love of beauty, her talent, and the support of family and friends, will live a fulfilling life.

A final book in this category, Patricia Beatty's *A Long Way to Whiskey Creek*, deserves mention. While it deals only tangentially with death, its humor and its earthy realism are a refreshing affirmation of life.

Parker Quiney is mean and tough. He doesn't do women's work, thank you. In fact, he doesn't take to women, especially his brother's wife, Nerissa. Parker can't read and is he proud of this ignorance! One doesn't need to read to become a bronco buster, his life's ambition.

Jonathan Graber is an orphan, the son of two schoolteachers, "wisdom bringers" in the words of Parker Quiney. Jonathan has long golden curls, speaks Spanish, and knows nothing about horses.

These two unlikely companions join together on a pilgrimage of four hundred miles over rough Texas land in the late 1800s, having suspenseful adventures, developing a friendship slowly and painfully and frequently humorously, and learning about life—and death.

Their mission is to bring back the body of Parker's older brother Jess, killed in a gunfight. Not wanting to travel alone, Parker gets Graber to accompany him, not because he likes Graber—he doesn't—but because he wants to rescue him from the clutches of the Widow Bybee, a mean old tyrant who makes money by housing orphans. The two boys argue constantly. Parker thinks Graber a sissy, a coward; Graber finds Parker an ignorant braggart. Together, however, although the two are slow to recognize it, they work well, drawing upon each other's strengths and learning from each other.

On their way, they meet up with a traveling medicine man, homesteaders, a Bible-thumping minister, prostitutes, an ex-convict, and other memorable but totally believable characters. They also meet the Petersons, the family of the man involved in the gunfight with Jess. Parker learns that both men were killed and, even more astonishing, that the men were friends. He is desperate to learn why they should have shot each other. The answer finally resolves one of the biggest conflicts Parker has with Graber: Parker is a Rebel, Graber a Yankee. When they discover that the fight was over who was the better general, Beauregard or Stuart, both Southern generals, and that such a silly quarrel led to the death of two young men, they realize how silly they are being.

> "There aren't any real Yankees any more or any more real Johnny Rebs. The war's been over for fourteen years. Won't anybody in Texas ever forget it?... We weren't even born yet when it had already ended" (198).

A final conflict they both face is a dread of digging up the body and a fear of haunting. Graber avoids the coffin they have brought along whenever he can. Finally, the ex-convict, the Tonkawa kid, tells them,

> "...dn' never be scared of nobody who's dead, colts. It's the livin' ones ya gotta be afeard of!" (206)

Thus, both Parker and Graber have grown up, having established a solid friendship, having learned from one another, and having gathered together the resources they need to live a happy, fulfilling life.

The most traumatic death a child has to face, with the exception of his own, is the death of a parent. Few books on this subject are available for younger children. While literature should help one deal with the less pleasant aspects of life, suggesting to a small child that he need prepare for the possible loss of a parent is foolhardy, causing unnecessary fear, worry, and stress. Only if a parent is terminally ill or if a parent dies unexpectedly should an adult use one of the books available.

One such book is Janice M. Hammond's *When My Dad Died: A Child's View of Death*. The author in her preface describes children as they respond to death and gives suggestions for adults. Likewise, at the end of the book is a bibliography of adult books on death. In the story itself, when a boy's father dies, he goes through the normal stages: He learns that death, unlike sleep, is permanent; he worries about who will take care of him (adjusting to his mother's having to work and finally understanding her obligation); he fears his mother, too, will die and is angry at his dad for leaving; even though he has once wished his father dead, he realizes that he is not responsible. The book emphasizes the need to communicate one's feelings. Through a helpful teacher and a loving mother, he realizes that he may laugh again, that he does not have to take his father's place, even that someday his mom may remarry. Although the author is guilty of gimmickry by making the book a coloring book (the child does not need secondary amusement), the sections at the end asking the child to write his own stories—"When my dad died, I felt," or "Sometimes I worry about"—would be immensely helpful if a child is having difficulty expressing his feelings.

Another helpful book for a young child who cannot reconcile the loss of a parent is *Sam, Bangs, and Moonshine* by Evaline Ness. Samantha, Sam for short, has not come to grips with the death of her mother. Although her father is a caring man, his job as a fisherman keeps him away a lot, and Sam has had to assume many of the household duties. To combat her grief and loneliness, Sam has created a rich fantasy world equipped with a magic carpet, a fierce lion as a pet, a baby kangaroo, and a mermaid mother. And she has marvelous conversations with her cat, Bangs.

A neighboring boy, Thomas, is a special friend, for he believes all her fantasies—"moonshine" as her father calls them. Each day Sam sends Thomas on treks to find her mythical kangaroo. One day, however, she sends Thomas to Blue Rock along with Bangs while she once again escapes into her own world. Unfortunately a sudden storm appears. No longer able to block out reality, Sam reveals all to her father when he comes home. He sets out immediately for Blue Rock—"'And pray that the tide hasn't covered the rock,'" he yells.

Sam's father does find Thomas, but Bangs appears to have drowned. That evening, her father tries to explain to Sam the difference between *real* and *moonshine*. "*Real* was no mother at all. *Real* was her father and Bangs. And now there wasn't even Bangs." Suddenly, she sees a "sodden mass" in the window. Bangs has returned. The next morning, she understands that there are good moonshine and bad moonshine. Her fantasies almost cost her both Thomas and Bangs.

Older children, of course, may face even more problems when a parent dies. These traumas include not only the reactions of a younger child, but also additional responsibilities and pressures. Two books do a fine job of showing life for a terminally ill parent and the resultant hardships for the entire family.

Although the dialogue in Patricia Hermes's *You Shouldn't Have to Say Good-Bye* is stilted, its characters undeveloped, and its subplot dealing with agoraphobia extraneous, the book gives valuable insights. Thirteen-year-old Sarah Morrow discovers that her mother is dying of a particularly virulent type of cancer, one that will take her quickly. Unlike the stalwart, controlled victims in other books, Mrs. Morrow has moments of severe depression mingled with anger. Sarah, of course, goes through the natural responses: anger, a need for denial, and misery. However, because of Mrs. Morrow's strength, the family members are able to salvage a great deal in their last few weeks together. Indeed, on the day of a Christmas party, all three realize separately that it is the happiest day of their lives.

Mrs. Morrow bargains, as so many terminal patients do, so that she has the strength both to attend a gymnastics meet important to Sarah and to last until Christmas Eve. In the meantime, she prepares the family to go on without her — she is teaching Sarah basic household chores like making decent coffee and doing laundry, and she purchases a multitude of books she hopes Sarah will read in the future. Most importantly, she keeps a diary for Sarah to read and treasure after her mother is dead.

The book ends three months after Mrs. Morrow's death. Although Sarah is not completely recovered, she is slowly learning to face life again, she and her father are growing even closer, and she is beginning to look forward to the future. Sarah knows that her mother's last words are right.

> I know I'm getting better. I know Daddy's going to get better.
> I know I'm growing up and learning a lot of things. And spring
> is coming, and I know I'm going to plant a garden. But I know
> something else. Mom is dead. And it stinks (117).

This book does not try to minimize the pain of the victim or her family and it does not flinch from the ultimate truth that losing a loved one will always "stink."

The Very Nearest Room by Jane Logan may be beneficial only in that the reader's life is probably so much happier than the protagonist's the reader will automatically feel better.

Lyn Kramer, at fifteen, has had an almost totally bleak existence. Since the birth of her younger brother, Peter, who is eight, their mother has been an invalid, having suffered a severe stroke during his birth. In the remainder of the book, she is to have several more, one necessitating a lengthy hospitalization and eventual institutionalization, the final one resulting in death. Since Lyn was thirteen, she has undertaken the care of her mother—a monumental task—and the rearing of Peter and their sister Alice, age thirteen.

The care of her mother is a burden. Not only is she cranky, but after another stroke, she becomes childlike, incontinent, unpredictable. The physical care alone would break most adults. But Lyn unflinchingly and uncomplainingly takes on the responsibility. When her mother must live in a nursing home, Lyn refuses to go see her—she feels abandoned. Even though caring for her mother has been dreadful, Lyn has always felt that she was at least a part of her mother's life.

Complicating the problems are her father and Peter. Mr. Kramer, a doctor, becomes immersed in his work. Away from home most of the time and despondent over his wife's illness, he turns the family over to Lyn. Although he realizes that he is being unfair to her, he is unable to take on the responsibilities himself. Peter presents even greater problems. Perhaps because he intuitively realizes that somehow his mother's illness resulted at his birth and he feels guilt, perhaps because he has been slight and weak from birth, perhaps because he is simply reacting to the unusual environment in which he has been reared, the child is strange, is therefore lonely, and is usually unhappy. The reader sees his desperation as he gets a kitten, the most unendearing animal anywhere in fiction, and loves it in spite of its nasty nature. When the cat falls ill and dies, Lyn is frantic over Peter's unrelieved grief and fears his never again being happy.

Lyn herself is a loner, spurning most of the time her younger sister, who is, admittedly, a rather shallow person caught up with boys, looks, and religion, but who is the most "normal" of the family. Nor does Lyn have any friends. Her only consolations are running and reading. By the end of the book, Lyn has tentatively made a friend, as has Peter, and we can rejoice in her strength and independence, but the book certainly paints a dismal picture of life.

It does, however, show great insight into the turmoil that can result from a terminally ill patient living at home. And when Lyn finally relents, going to see her mother, who will not last through the night, we see the toll that her mother's death will bring.

A book dealing with an unusual and dangerous reaction to a parent's death is *Remember Me When I Am Dead* by Carol Beach York. Because of the brooding suspense of this book, because of its rather sophisticated insights into human behavior, and because of its chilling conclusion, it requires a reader who is both perceptive and insightful. Atypically, the book does not concentrate on the child characters alone, but delves into the minds of the adults as well, giving the child reader an unusual perspective.

After Evelyn Loring dies, her husband remarries. His new wife, Margaret, is a loving woman who is surrounded by conflict and doubt. She is trying to fit in, she is certainly aware of all the memories of Evelyn that still cling, and she and her husband both are legitimately concerned over the well-being of the younger daughter, Jenny. Complicating matters is the upcoming Christmas holiday, the first Christmas the children will spend with their new mother.

On the last day of school before vacation, Jenny rushes in, ecstatic because she thinks she has caught a glimpse of Mr. Hoffman, a friend of their mother's, who returned to Germany after her death. The adults are worried that his reappearance will reopen old wounds for Jenny. While eleven-year-old Sara was able to grieve openly for her mother, Jenny still has not been able to accept the reality of her mother's death. Suddenly, strange occurrences begin. The parents find in one of Jenny's books a poem:

> Roses are blue
> Violets are red
> Remember me
> When I am dead.
> 　　　　　Momma.

Two days later, they find a letter addressed to Evelyn, waiting to be mailed. They begin to wonder if they should send Jenny away to school, to provide her with a new environment so that she will begin to adjust. Mrs. Dow, the housekeeper, finds a bunch of mistletoe crudely taped to the archway, a tradition of Evelyn's. And on Christmas morning, a package appears under the tree, a cheap bottle of perfume for Jenny from "Momma."

At first, we wonder if indeed these occurrences are supernatural, but quickly realize that Jenny must be acting out her innermost agonies. Jenny is a delightful child, a "small elfin girl" full of energy and love. Because she is so delightful, adults, even her parents, are unable to avoid favoring her over her prim, rather plain older sister. The reader sees the problems caused by her not expressing her grief, and fears permanent emotional damage.

In the startling conclusion, however, we find that it is Sara who has manufactured the notes, the present, the mistletoe. She, too, has not purged herself of her mother's memory — not loving remembrances for her, but a hateful resentment that her mother always cared more for Jenny than for her. She believes that if Jenny is sent away to school, "Margaret and Daddy would love Sara; she would be all they had...."

When Sara finds out that indeed Jenny will be sent away to school, that her plan has worked, she is shocked to discover that she, too, will be going away so that Jenny will not be lonely. She realizes then that Margaret and Daddy and Mrs. Dow do love her, but what can she do? If she confesses, no one will love her.

> Sara felt a small hand touch hers, and she looked down into Jenny's tearful eyes.

Gazing up into the face of the person in the world she should least trust, Jenny said with little sobs: "I'm glad you're going too, Sara. I don't want to go alone."

As we read these last lines of the book, we realize that unresolved bitterness at a person who has died can warp one, as can unresolved love for that person. Not only Sara's fate but Jenny's as well—at the hands of Sara—looks bleak indeed.

Also destructive is denial. Three books do a particularly good job of exploring this problem. Because of the sophistication of the first-person narrator, *A Season In-Between* demands an older, more mature reader. Carrie is a bright but insecure girl who copes with the world through sarcasm and a self-effacing humor. Indeed, her observations about herself and others are frequently hilarious. Perhaps her relationship with her younger brother best illustrates her nature. While she continually refers to him as "The Brat" and constantly needles him, her real concern for him shows clearly. When Sonny becomes difficult to handle as a result of their father's terminal illness, it is Carrie who tolerates him, defends him, protects him.

Much of Carrie's conflict, of course, centers around her father's illness and impending death. She longs to be in control as her mother is and thus refuses to cry. At first, she also refuses to confront her father. She pays dutiful visits to him in his room but is bothered by his paleness and the smell of medicine. Finally, an acquaintance, a girl whom Carrie has never really cared for, reveals that her mother has had a mastectomy and offers to talk to Carrie if Carrie ever needs a friend: "'I know how awful it is and no one ever wants to talk about it'" (78). Eventually Carrie is able to relate once more to her father. One night, they take a long walk together, and they are able to discuss his illness openly.

Like so many cancer victims, Carrie's father has one last burst of energy, enabling the family to have a night out at the club; the next morning he must return to the hospital. A few days later, he dies. The days and weeks that follow are particularly rough. Even Carrie's mother, always in control, fumbles through the days. Once more, Sonny comes to the rescue, giving Carrie something to focus on and finally helping her accept the finality of death: "'What's left is what we remember, all the good times, all the wonderful things he did with us '" (122). She, in turn, assures him that he will not be a sissy if he cries. Her mother, too, finally takes hold, and as she and Carrie become involved in the family business, they begin to establish a new pattern, a renewed family life, and Carrie herself is becoming more comfortable socially with her friends and with boys as well.

The title of *A Formal Feeling* by Zibby Oneal is an allusion to an Emily Dickinson poem that explores the natural process of grief. Unfortunately, the protagonist, Anne Cameron, has not progressed beyond the first stage, the "formal feeling" that leaves one numb, unable to express true emotions. It is over a year now since her mother has died, and Anne has cried only once. She ignores her feelings by dealing with others only superficially, by running cross-country or ice skating until she has obliterated all feelings.

This Christmas vacation, when she returns home from boarding school, is particularly difficult for Anne because her father has remarried. Anne is confused because her older brother Spencer not only seems to accept his new stepmother but does not have the same feelings she has toward their mother. In addition, Anne is unable to communicate with her lifelong friend, Laura, or a boy she has formerly been interested in. Her term paper simply won't materialize, and she is haunted by blanks in her past. It is not until she remembers that her mother left the family—to "find space"—when Anne was only eight that Anne is able to admit that her mother was often overbearing, often demanding, not allowing anyone to have imperfections. "She knew the question had always been there, unspeakable, at the bottom of all she remembered and had chosen to forget. And she made herself ask: Did I ever love my mother at all?" (155). She finally realizes that yes, she loved her mother. "They had loved each other in their imperfect ways. And it was all right" (156). Now Anne may grieve for her mother for who she was and can begin to live her life again.

In *A Matter of Time* by Roni Schotter, Lisl Gilbert's mother is dying of cancer. A routine operation becomes a death sentence, and the entire family must cope. Lisl's father cannot reveal his feelings and becomes even more withdrawn. Lisl's older sister Jane and Jane's husband, Jim, are supportive but have their own lives to live in another city. And Lisl is torn apart. She has always envied her mother, even been jealous of her, since her mother is beautiful, talented, and charming, while Lisl considers herself a "nothing." To protect herself, Lisl builds a wall, refusing to tell any of her friends, refusing to let anything touch her.

Finally, however, she cannot hide the truth from anyone—her mother's deterioration is too obvious. Further, she must explain her behavior to her friends and her teachers. The real breakthrough occurs when she is able to see her mother as a vulnerable, helpless human being. A simple contribution of finding a way for her mother to wear a scarf to hide the marks of treatment brings Lisl and her mother together. The entire family rallies, and when Mrs. Gilbert is hospitalized and dies, Lisl is able to say to her,

> ...one last time ... I love you. I always will. I guess in a lot of ways we never really understood each other all that well.... I wish you could have stayed around longer so we could have gotten to know each other better (125-6).

As she cries, "the saddest and deepest tears I had ever cried," she feels better, "as if I'd been cleaned out" (126).

While the treatment of death in this novel is somewhat mechanical, it does offer two important insights. After Lisl's friends learn of her mother's illness, they make her miserable in trying to be considerate:

> It was all a foolish and misguided attempt to spare my feelings and cheer me up. Whenever I appeared, there was an immediate hush followed by lots of mad merriment.... The worst of it was that somewhere along the line the word "dead" and all words associated with it magically dropped out of the English language.... My friends had purged all such words from their vocabularies (44-5).

Finally, Lisl is furious: "This cancer business was interfering with *everything*. At home, life seemed dark and unreal. And now I couldn't even have a real laugh with a real friend" (45). When she blows up at her friends, they stop the phoniness and actually become a real comfort to her.

Another important insight is the help available through counseling. When Jane and Jim invite a social worker in to talk with the entire family, Lisl resists with determination. Later, however, she seeks out the woman, who is able to help her through the ordeal.

Sometimes it is the remaining parent's inability to cope that causes undue pressure. *Ronnie and Rosey* by Judie Angell is somewhat uneven in quality. During the first section, when a girl named Ronnie, having just moved into a new neighborhood, makes friends with Evelyn, Rosey (short for Robert Rose), and Miss Fisk, the gym teacher, the plot revolves around some trivial events and is sometimes tedious. When Ronnie's father dies, however, the book becomes both suspenseful and meaningful. The basic conflict occurs between Ronnie, who is becoming more and more involved romantically with Rosey, and her mother, who simply cannot adjust to her husband's death. First, she becomes totally dependent on Ronnie, pleading with her to remain home from school, discouraging her from attending any social events. The mother is becoming more and more withdrawn, ignoring friends and even her painting, once a focal point of her life.

Later, this dependency turns into possessiveness. Ronnie's mother deeply resents Ronnie's relationship with Rosey. Soon, she is making impossible rules, forbidding them to see each other except at school and limiting their phone conversations to ten minutes. When Ronnie and Rosey resort to sneaking around and lying, they are caught each time. In addition, Ronnie begins to develop severe headaches, both because of her guilt over lying to her mother and because of her unresolved grief.

The main insight in the book is the incredible damage unresolved grief can bring about. Because Ronnie and her mother never discuss their loss, because both are cut off from friends, willingly or not, not only do they not express their grief, but they also contain the anger both feel at the "abandonment" of husband and father.

Not until Miss Fisk intervenes do the two of them finally talk and realize that they have been taking out all their guilt and hurt on each other. The change in Ronnie's mother is rather abrupt; nevertheless, the two begin to reestablish the loving relationship they had in the past.

The protagonist of *Sometimes I Don't Love My Mother* by Hila Colman suffers a similar fate. After Dallas's father dies, her mother is unable to adjust. To compensate for her loss, Mrs. Davis becomes overprotective of Dallas, overreliant on her. Having recently graduated from high school, Dallas agrees not to go away to college as planned. Soon, she discovers that even a trip to the library is unacceptable. Further, as Dallas begins to have friends over and insists that she be allowed to go places, Mrs. Davis, in turn, insists upon being included. Dallas even suspects her mother of having designs on Victor, a boy whom Dallas is beginning to love. All of these pressures make Dallas question her love for her mother. Not until Mrs. Davis's own mother visits, a woman who has always tried to dominate *her* life, does Mrs. Davis realize what she has been doing over the months, and a reconciliation begins.

This book has few redeeming features. First of all, the narrative technique is inconsistent. Told primarily from Dallas's point of view, the book makes promises it cannot fulfill when twice it delves into the mind of the mother. Equally disturbing is the didacticism; the book tells the message instead of showing it. And as a treatise on grief, it falls short. The dead father is a stick figure. We find only that the two characters miss him, but we are not sure why (his sole function in life appears to have been arranging parties and doing household chores). We are told that the characters miss him and that the grief process lasts a long time. The only real insight occurs during the funeral when Dallas fears that her father is not really dead: "What if he came out of the coma? What if he couldn't get out?" (15), a typical reaction of bereaved persons.

Because sex appears briefly in the book, some girls might want to read it. Otherwise, it is a simplistic, typical piece of adolescent fiction.

Certain characteristics usually mark Mary Stolz's books: She emphasizes the beauty of nature and the grandeur of animal life; she is a strong advocate of ecology; and the endings of her books are open-ended. *The Edge of Next Year* is harsh in its realities.

Orin Woodward loses his mother when he is fourteen. Because both his parents are orphans, no relatives exist to help out. Because of his mother's independence and reclusiveness, the family has isolated itself, content with its own harmony, and thus no close friends are available either. Most of the burden falls upon Orin.

His younger brother Victor is loveable but strange. He cares far more for nature's creatures than human beings. To deal with his grief and the family problems, Victor immerses himself more and more with his "friends," surrounding himself with snakes, turtles, lizards, and insects. While Orin understands his little brother and loves him, Victor's withdrawal does little to help Orin find comfort. Perhaps even more devastating is Mr. Woodward's reaction:

Unable to cope with the loss of his wife or the responsibilities of running a household, he turns to alcohol. As the novel progresses, his problem worsens so that eventually he is consuming nearly a fifth of liquor a day. Worried and yet disgusted over his father's problem, Orin must also run the household. These chores leave him no time to participate in sports at school or to develop outside friendships. Essentially, Orin is alone in his grief and struggles to overcome it.

Two breakthroughs do finally occur. One day, totally fed up with his father, Orin agrees to take Victor to the caves, an expedition Orin finds both dangerous and terrifying. While Victor is fascinated underground, Orin is totally miserable. When they finally reach air and light again, Orin finds that he is experiencing great joy: "'I think I never realized before what it's like, just being under the sky. . . . Oh, you are one marvelous world,' he crowed" (188). And when they return home, their father tells them that he is joining Alcoholics Anonymous. Does Orin dare to hope? He decides, "You could be optimistic, if you wanted to be. He felt optimistic now. He didn't know how it was going to turn out. Who ever knew how things would work out?" (194). He realizes that he still misses his mother, but "You got on with your life. And if you were alive, you had to be happy sometimes, and care about things" (194–5).

The responsibilities that Orin must assume are a frequent burden for children who have lost a parent. In *Pennies for the Piper* by Susan McLean, for instance, the reader may be somewhat skeptical at first. Although the main character, Bicks (Victoria Purvis), is streetwise, having lived a period of time in the inner city of Minneapolis, she is, after all, only ten and thus not wise enough or strong enough to endure or to perceive as she does. Soon, however, the reader does believe that "'Little Purvis can take care of herself. Independent as they come. . . . She's a cool one, little Purvis'" (124–5).

During the course of the book, Bicks has four major challenges. At the first, caring for her ill mother and the needs of their existence, she has become expert. In addition, she must worry about her younger friend, Stubbs, a boy cursed with a mentally ill mother who abuses him, neglects him, and eventually throws him out. He seeks refuge with Bicks and her mother until his older sister Stace rescues him. The central conflict, of course, is the impending and eventual death of Bicks's mother. Mrs. Purvis has everything arranged: her funeral paid for, and money under her pillow that Bicks is to use to ride the bus to Dubuque to live with her Aunt Millicent after her mother's death. The reader sees the natural fear Bicks experiences each time her mother's breathing changes or she grimaces in pain. And he also sees her resistance to any adult help: She lies to the nosy neighbor downstairs, to her Aunt Millicent who calls long distance, to a caring teacher.

Thus when Bicks returns home one day after school to find her mother dead, she determines to make all the arrangements herself. Remarkably, she calls the funeral home, packs up their few belongings to be sent along to Dubuque, and decides that she must stay for the funeral to pay her last respects to the mother she has loved so much. In purchasing a lovely burial wreath, she must use part of her precious bus fare. Thus, after the ceremony, Bicks sets out to walk from Minneapolis to Dubuque. The suspense is tremendous here as various friends and acquaintances in Minneapolis—her teacher, the funeral director, Stace and Stubbs—help unravel the mystery of Bicks's whereabouts from the time her mother dies on Monday to the funeral on Thursday, and as Bicks herself attempts her long walk. Meanwhile, Aunt Millicent becomes aware of all the events and is beside herself with worry over her small niece.

The book is well worth reading for its marvelous plot and its true-to-life, frequently endearing characters. It is additionally valuable because of its insights into death. Because Bicks has known for months that her mother is to die, she is somewhat prepared for the tragedy and is certainly able to handle all the practical aspects. She delays her grief, however, and suffers greatly. "She would not cry. Would not, in any way, betray her grief" (102). In spite of the fact that she has disobeyed her mother's wishes, she knows that her mother would understand, that Bicks cannot "go away and leave Mums lying there all alone—not knowing when she'd be buried, or worse yet, whether she'd be buried in the right place with no one to watch. . . . It would've been too hard for her to just walk away as Mums had told her to do" (102). At the cemetery, however, after everyone has left, she breaks down. The reader sees this sensitivity in her collecting lilacs from a neighbor, putting them in fruit jars, and placing the containers on neglected graves in a nearby cemetery. She hopes that someone will do the same for her mother.

Most of all, she rejoices that she has paid the piper, that she has seen the the ordeal through herself: "Unshared. A precious farewell. . . . To share it would diminish it. It had been her own" (145). When she reaches her Aunt Millicent, when she realizes what love and comfort await her there, she knows that she is truly home. "There was still sorrow and tears. With time it would be less heavy" (146).

When the parents of Bill, Lori, and Kevin Keller are killed in a plane crash, the protagonists of *When the Phone Rang* by Harry Mazer face innumerable problems. At Billy's insistence, Kevin quits college, returns home, and attempts to hold the family together both financially and emotionally. Other relatives are skeptical about the arrangement, and throughout, a social worker's interest in their progress threatens their security.

Several keen insights into death appear. At first, both because of grief and because of lack of guidance, the three lead a Bohemian existence. Lori and Billy don't return to school for several weeks, the house becomes a shambles, they keep no routine, and they exist on junk food. Lori and Billy have an especially difficult time when they do return to school, totally uncomfortable over the words of comfort and encouragement their teachers and classmates try to offer. Neither Billy nor Lori can stand any changes in the house. When Kevin insists upon moving into their parents' room so that he can have privacy and a place to study, the younger children are angry and hurt. Each child has his own demons as well—Billy continues to deny his parents' deaths, clinging stubbornly to the belief that one day they will be there when he returns from school; Lori is perhaps the most devastated, turning in her loneliness to an unsuitable friend who lies and shoplifts; Kevin resents his responsibilities and the necessity of being away from his girlfriend, who lives in Boston. Eventually, the three survive, finally finding focus in their lives, solving the practical problems, and becoming closer.

Although the conflicts may be resolved a bit too neatly in *The Gift of the Pirate Queen* by Patricia Reilly Giff, this book has real merit in showing the long-term effects when a child loses a parent. The main character, Grace, has several problems. First, she worries constantly about her younger sister Amy, who has diabetes and will not stick to her diet. While the reader understands the difficulty a child has in resisting sweets, he, like Grace, becomes furious when

Amy sneaks sweets or wheedles them out of others. The reader also sees the effects of too little insulin and too much insulin in separate incidents.

In addition, Grace has broken a beautiful Christmas bell of her teacher's, a woman who appears cold and unfeeling. In trying to cover her tracks, Grace is unfair to a classmate, Lisa, whom she feels sorry for but finds difficult to like because Lisa is dirty and irresponsible.

The biggest problem Grace faces is the arrival of a cousin from Ireland, Fiona, who Grace fears will stay forever and attempt to replace Grace's mother, who died the year before. Grace misses her mother constantly, yet she is terrified because she can no longer clearly remember her mother's face or her voice.

While the other conflicts work out a bit too smoothly, this last conflict has a believable resolution. Because Fiona is a warm, loving, and wise person, she slowly and carefully becomes an integral part of the household. She is careful not to disrupt any of the old patterns, keeping the memory of the mother alive for the children and patiently giving comfort and love to the family. By the end of the novel, Grace willingly accepts from Fiona the love and guidance she so desperately needs. Now she can be a child again.

In *Where the Lilies Bloom* by Vera and Bill Cleaver, the authors once again deal with an Appalachian family, poor, largely uneducated, but wise and gutsy. Mary Call, the protagonist, is a feisty survivor who at thirteen overcomes formidable obstacles; her character is so strong, however, that the reader readily accepts her victories.

Mary Call's father is ill, and when he has a stroke both he and Mary Call know that his time is short. He extracts from her several promises: she is not to call a doctor; she is to give him a simple burial in the mountains; she is to keep the family together at whatever cost; and she is not to allow her sister, Devola, whom Mary Call calls "cloudy-headed," to marry their landlord, Kiser Pease.

Mary, Devola, ten-year-old Romey, and Ima Dean, not yet of school age, struggle to keep the family going. Because they fear "do-gooders" who may put them in an institution, they hide their father's illness and later his death. Seizing upon an opportunity, they nurse Kiser back to health in return for a paper signing over their home and twenty acres to them. At the same time, they take up "wildcrafting," the harvesting of buds, roots, leaves, and bark to sell to pharmaceutical companies. After the father dies, conditions worsen. Not only must they continue to deceive the neighbors into thinking that their father is still alive, Mary must constantly fend off Kiser, who is obviously in love with Devola. Although they manage to accumulate enough food for the winter, the house is in deplorable shape, and the weather is fierce. Finally, in desperation, Mary Call offers herself in marriage to Kiser, since she finds that the paper he has signed not legal and since Kiser's sister is preparing to kick the family off the place. Kiser turns out not to be the ogre Mary Call has thought him, and Devola unexpectedly takes charge, marrying Kiser herself; she now looks "deep and strong with a kind of grand, maternal dignity" (162). Now the entire burden of the family will no longer rest on Mary Call.

The book does an excellent job in dealing with problems surrounding death. Although tough and reliable, Mary Call is really too young to take on the enormous responsibilities of the family. When their father dies, she and Romey go through a grueling ordeal in order to bury him as he has requested, trudging miles over rough terrain, pulling their father in Romey's wagon. And because they must keep his death a secret, all four children must contain their grief, making eventual acceptance even harder. The major insight, however, concerns the promises Mary Call has made. "'Seems to me,' remarked Kiser in an offhand way, 'like Roby Luther put a lot off on to you that didn't belong'" (163). While Mary Call protests, she knows that Kiser is right. Both she and her father had obviously misjudged Devola, who should rightfully marry Kiser, and the family must not turn down help out of foolish pride.

Other books also stress the practical hardships the entire family must face when a parent dies. *A Little Destiny* by Vera and Bill Cleaver is compelling, well-written—and totally preposterous. Taking place somewhere in the South during the early part of the twentieth century, the story traces the movements of Lucy Commander, her brother Lyman, and their mother after the sudden death of Mr. Commander. Lucy discovers immediately that when her father was attacked by a yearling horse, and their servant, Marion, tried to go to his rescue, Tom Clegg prevented Marion's assistance. The only explanation offered is that Tom Clegg had wanted to marry Lucy's mother when she married Mr. Commander instead. Further complications arise when the family find that they are in Tom Clegg's debt. When he proposes marriage to the mother and she refuses, he calls in the debts, forcing them to move into town and eke out a living. Lyman, a doctor practicing in another town, must move home to care for his mother and sister. When an itinerant joins with the family and helps them restore neglected family property, luck seems to be changing. However, the evil Tom Clegg arranges for the kidnapping of both Lyman and Lucy. What follows— ambushes, gunplay, and an attempt by Lucy to kill her avowed enemy—is straight from an old, tired Western.

The book does a good job of showing the practical obstacles frequently facing the family after a death, but the reader doesn't really see the normal stages of grief. Lucy is more bent on exacting revenge than on remembering her father.

Far better treatment of practical matters comes in *The Summer After the Funeral* by Jane Gardam. An elderly rector has died, leaving behind his widow and their three children, Athene, Sebastian, and Beams, nee Phoebe. What follows is a story of adventure, suspense, sensitivity, and rollicking fun. As the reader follows the lives of the four survivors, he sees not only the impact of the rector's death, but the impact of his life on them. Offered also are contrasting views of both parents.

Mrs. Price, left destitute, must find a place to live and means to support the family. She foists the children off on unsuspecting friends and relatives and gallivants around England in search of a home. We see her activities through the letters she writes. What emerges is an often thoughtless, normally scatterbrained woman who ignores Beams, embarrasses Athene, and wins the adoration of her son. Underneath, she is a lovely woman, willing to serve, generous to a fault.

Sebastian is the stoic of the family. He chooses to spend his time in retreat at an abbey, where the calm and the discipline soothe his soul. He chooses to tell his family that he is going to a Buddhist commune in Scotland. He befriends Lucien, an older boy, and finally is able to reveal his "sin" to the head of the abbey: Sebastian has always detested his father, a man adored by most women and one who obviously preferred his daughters to his son. Thus Sebastian has come to worship his mother; he sees her almost as a martyr, wearing herself out in service to her husband and family.

Beams, the youngest child, is staying with the family of a school acquaintance. This family could delicately be called "robust" both in size and in activity. We see more of Beams's past than Sebastian's. Endowed with a superior intellect and pushed by both her parents from early childhood, Beams reacts emotionally, being unable to read most of her life. The parents have taken her to a series of psychiatrists, most of them preposterous. Finally, they find an effective one who helps her overcome her barriers. Likewise, she begins to accept her ugliness (the other children are comely), begins to use her amazing brain, and rids herself of the jealousy she has always felt for Athene.

Athene is the major character of the story. Ashamed of her father's advanced age, embarrassed by her mother's vulgarity, Athene does not know who she is and fears that she is losing her mind. The variety of names she is called throughout indicates her lack of identity, and the places she is sent lead her into wild adventures, all again indicating her search for a niche in life. During her stay at Cousin Posie's, Athene spies and becomes enthralled with a mysterious young man who reminds her of Heathcliff in *Wuthering Heights*. Next she goes to visit Sybil, an old family friend who is hysterical most of the time and who lives with an old harridan whom Athene hates immediately. Running away, she spends the night at the home of a middle-aged artist, a real Bohemian who is enthralled by her beauty but whom she suspects of lustful thoughts. She runs away from him as well, making her way to her aunt's school. Because she is early, her aunt is away, and only one teacher is left as a caretaker. He and Athene become friends and she begins to love him, but she finds that he is married. Once again she runs away.

The plot becomes more and more entangled as the entire family realize that Athene is missing. In a wild series of circumstances, all of the characters in the book end up at the old manse, hoping to find Athene. They find her at the top of the tower. They believe she is going to jump, but actually, she is simply looking at her father's grave, trying to say good-bye to her old life. The entire family decide that they do not wish to live at the rectory with their mother as housekeeper. Instead, she will be a housemother at Aunt Boo's school, where, incidentally, Lucien will be (he turns out to be the Heathcliff look-alike), and all are happy.

Three books deal with the terror a parental death can induce. A typical and devastating terror is the fear of abandonment. The major focus of *The Year the Dreams Came Back* by Anita Macrae Feagles is the lack of understanding between parents and children, a natural questioning of parental values, mannerisms, and attitudes. Nell's three friends, Gwynn, Gordie, and Nancy, have totally different parents from Nell and from each other—and all complain. Nell envies them for some parts of their lives and is secretly glad that she does not have to share other parts. During the course of the novel, she realizes that Gwynn is not really the friend she has wanted, while she grows closer to Nancy and develops a romantic interest in Gordie. Nell's major problem, however, is her inability to accept her mother's suicide the previous year. She and her father—the "Giant Crab"—have an uneasy truce. Likewise, visits from her maternal grandmother put both of them out of sorts. Her father has struggled for years with her mother's depression and is struggling now to pull himself out of the debt all the hospitalization brought about. Unfortunately, neither one of them is able to talk about the tragedy in their lives or the guilt each feels—what didn't they do that they should have? When Nell befriends a newcomer in town, Amy, and introduces her to her father, the three quickly become friends. Little does Nell realize that eventually Amy and her father will fall in love and wish to marry.

When she finds out their plans, Nell runs away. When Gordie asks her why she opposes the marriage she rejects all the normal answers—jealousy, loyalty to her mother, anger. Finally, she realizes she is experiencing fear, fear that Amy, too, will kill herself after living with Nell and her father. At last her guilt has surfaced. When she discusses her feelings with Amy, Nell knows that she can now accept both her mother's death and her father's upcoming marriage. The nightmares of the last year can now become dreams once more, dreams of a happy future.

Sister by Eloise Greenfield does not end as happily. Doretha, at thirteen, has had to face some grim realities during her short life. At present, her most pressing problem is her older sister, Alberta, who has taken to the streets, causing grief for their mother, for obvious reasons, and for Doretha, who has deep compassion for her mother's distress, fears for her sister's future, and worries that she, too, will one day follow in her sister's footsteps. Through a series of flashbacks, we find the reasons for Alberta's confusion and misery.

Subtly, the author shows the cruelties connected with life in the inner city: indifferent landlords, frequent hunger, demeaning labor with little respect. No wonder Alberta has taken to the streets to escape. In addition, Alberta has never recovered from the sudden death of her father, three years before. Intuitively realizing her sister's despair, Doretha has promised her sister, "'Alberta, I won't never go away. I promise. I won't never, never leave you'" (34). Doretha knows that Alberta feels deserted by her father.

Doretha also has typical problems of adolescence. At school, she is saddled with an uncaring, often cruel teacher who makes Doretha feel dumb, who sets up a self-fulfilling prophecy for the child who falls further and further behind. Doretha is also beginning to discover boys and must handle her mixed emotions of attraction and fear. When she attends a concert of a current rock band, she romantically expects the lead singer to pick her out of the crowd, to love her instantly, to give her recognition, a fantasy showing her desperate need to escape her environment.

Throughout, however, Doretha has many positive influences. She and her mother are truly close, other family members give aid and support, and she has become involved with a black freedom organization that gives her identity. It is her grandfather's story of *his* grandfather that gives her the most strength, a man who was "'Fighting the pain, yes, sir! Fighting it and laughing at it'" (65). Using this heritage, Doretha will avoid Alberta's taking to the street to "'laugh all the time. At everything . . . and I don't get lonesome, and don't nobody hurt my feelings, 'cause I'm too busy laughing and having fun'" (78-9); instead, Doretha will "remember most . . . the good times, the family and friend times, the love times, that rainbowed their way way through the hard times" (82). She realizes that she is herself, *not* Alberta, but that even Alberta could be helped, that Doretha would "start showing her what she had seen" (82).

A Sound of Chariots by Mollie Hunter deals with another type of terror – the terror of death. The book is marvelous in its insights, in its style. However, the sophisticated style limits the readership to truly mature readers, as does the complicated handling of religion and politics. Bridie, in her early years from nine to twelve, although sensitive and bright, could not have the perceptions she is credited with. Nevertheless, the book does offer some keen insights into death.

The first part of the book establishes Bridie's relationships with the other members of the family. Her three older sisters she simply refers to as "The Others." Only her little brother, William, is she truly close to. And while her mother is a sweet and loving woman, it is Bridie's father who is the center of Bridie's existence, a fact that causes some resentment in her mother. Even while he is alive, life is harsh. Having been hurt in the First World War, Mr. McShane barely ekes out a living; the family lives in the War Parish and is thus surrounded by the war wounded, men without arms or legs. When Bridie's father dies, the problems worsen. Money is a constant worry, the menial jobs Mrs. McShane must take make her prematurely old, and eventually all the children must take positions elsewhere as they grow up, forsaking any hope of education.

Because of her father's death and the subsequent treatment Bridie receives, she becomes preoccupied with the temporary nature of life; she hears at her back "Time's winged chariot hurrying near." The mother's grief is unrestrained. Not even her fundamentalist religion helps, and she cries out, "'There's no God! *There's no God!*'" (123). None of the children find release from their grief, and Bridie becomes terrified of death, troubled by nightmares, and consumed by despair. The only comfort she finds is in words and literature, finally embracing poetry as a comfort and an outlet as she begins to express her innermost thoughts. Although she does find some mentors along the way, and although she does realize how much she loves and respects her mother, Bridie does not come to grips with death until she is able to open up to her teacher, Dr. McIntyre, who tells her,

> "All men are afraid of the passage of Time carrying them on to death, but ... there are only a few who have the talent to express their awareness in some creative form ... you will learn, you *must* learn, to build consciously, creatively outwards from it" (238).

He also reminds her that she must live for her father: "'You are your father's daughter. He's in your brain and in your blood. Live for him! Don't let your talent die because he is dead. Let it flower from his death and speak for both of you'" (238).

Most of these books thus far deal with extreme reactions. Others show that even normal grief is difficult, particularly when an extremely close relationship existed between the child and the parent he has lost.

In *There Are Two Kinds of Terrible* by Peggy Mann, Robbie loves his mother. She is always there; she always knows what to do; she is his best friend. While he loves his father ("He's my father, after all. And he's always been perfectly nice to me" [18]), the two do not communicate; his father is, in Robbie's words, a cold fish. When Robbie breaks his arm on the first day of summer vacation, he feels that he has experienced the worst. Because his injury requires surgery, he must wear a cast the entire summer — no tennis, no practice on his drums, no swimming. Robbie is actually glad when school starts again in the fall. Soon he is to learn a valuable but painful lesson:

> There are two kinds of terrible. The first is regular-trouble. It can happen to anyone. Any time. Like me breaking my right arm at the beginning of summer vacation.... Then there's this other kind of terrible — which makes the first kind shrink into nothing at all. The second kind has no end. And it's so much worse that there hasn't been any word invented for it. At least, no word that I know (61).

Robbie's mother goes into the hospital for tests. Women kind, she tells him. Then she must have a minor operation. After weeks when she still hasn't been released from the hospital, his dad tells Robbie what Robbie has suspected but not admitted: His mother has cancer. In fact, her virulent illness kills her in just two days after Robbie is allowed to visit her.

Most of what Robbie experiences is typical. He stresses his lack of reality during visitation and during the funeral. It is not until he hears the dirt hit his mother's casket that he begins sobbing, running blindly through the cemetery. He experiences great discomfort at school around the other children.

> It was like I had suddenly turned into some kind of freak or something. No one in the class had ever had a mother that died.

And no one had told them how they should act.... It really hurt me when people asked me about her. Yet, on the other hand, I'm glad they did (82).

Later, he feels great hatred for his mother. His Aunt Emily tells him that when his mother first began to experience pain, she refused to see a doctor. "If she'd gone earlier," Robbie thinks, "when the pains began, maybe she wouldn't have had to die and leave me all alone" (107).

His biggest problem, however, is his aloneness. He is an only child; the few relatives his family has live far away; and his father has built around himself an even thicker shell. Except for a brief moment on the way home from the hospital after Robbie's only visit to his mother, when his father pulls the car off the road and he and Robbie cling together, crying, no communication exists. The days and weeks after are a nightmare. It is not until Robbie discovers a picture album and realizes that his father's grief is far greater than his own that he is able to reach out to his father. At the end of the story, the two have a long way to go, but they have taken that first tentative step toward becoming a loving family of two.

While the protagonist of *The Empty Chair* by Bess Kaplan is ten, only an older reader can appreciate all of the irony and the humor in the book. When Becky's mother becomes pregnant, Becky is overjoyed at the prospect of having a baby sister (she just knows the baby will be a girl). However, both the mother and the baby die during childbirth, leaving Becky, her brother Saul, and her father alone. In step the relatives, aunties and cousins, to find another wife for Mr. Devine. The bickering, the manipulation, the jealousies and the shenanigans of these female matchmakers provide hilarity. In addition, only an older reader can appreciate the picture the author paints of life in the Depression.

A ten-year-old can, however, relate to Becky and her suffering as a result of her mother's death. The days following the death are poignant. Immediately, Becky is fiercely loyal to her mother's memory, screaming at an uncle who has dared to sit in her mother's chair, rescuing her mother's apron and mixing spoon so that no one can use them. Later, when the matchmaking begins, Becky is sure that her mother will not allow Papa to remarry. Although Becky is certainly old enough to realize that her mother is dead, she really does not come to grips with reality for over a year. Then, when her father *does* remarry, Becky is torn, angry and confused. While she comes to love and respect her stepmother, Sylvia, she still feels like a traitor. Soon, she begins to think her mother is angry and is trying to hurt the entire family for their betrayal. When her father falls and breaks a leg, Becky is sure that her mother is responsible, and then she begins to fear for her own safety.

Much of the book is devoted to the normal events in a growing child's life: altercations with a younger sibling, the need to be like other children, uncertainty about the future, misconceptions and questions about sex, worries about physical appearance. Throughout, Becky learns to adjust to a myriad of relatives and classmates with all of their idiosyncracies.

It is not until she finally reveals her fears to her parents that the major problem begins to resolve itself. Her well-meaning father did not allow her to attend the funeral. When he takes her to the cemetery, finally, to visit her mother's grave, she realizes:

> Mama was here underneath the snow and the earth. She had been here since the first minute. She was never in my head or my heart or my stomach. She wasn't in my bedroom or at the beach or anyplace. Just here. She had been here all along, I thought, under the snow. (236)

Becky also realizes that her mother always loved her, but is now resting in peace.

Lack of communication is also a major problem in *Grover* by Vera and Bill Cleaver. This excellent novel follows the illness of Grover's mother, her suicide, and the painful attempt he and his father make to cope and survive.

When his mother is hospitalized, Grover's father is devastated but cannot communicate his agony.

> He is a good man, my father, thought Grover, but were anybody to ask me if I wanted to be like him I would have to say no because with everything and everybody except my mother he is sketchy. He doesn't look at things or listen. It strains him to talk to people (12).

Nor can Grover confide in others.

> He asked his anxious questions but the smooth answers cheated
> him. The half-truths in them had good intentions but they
> didn't help the anxiety and they left him with a still anger. They
> didn't help the fear that hung in his mind (25).

When Grover's mother returns from the hospital, he feels that
life will be normal again, but he is confused that his mother wants
so much of his time. Like a typical boy, he would prefer going about
his business. One talk, however, is to remain forever with him. His
mother has told him that he is more a Cornett than Ezell, taking
more after her side of the family, and "'Cornetts don't howl about
things'" (66), but she assures him that his father, too, is "'equal to
any situation.'" Not suprisingly, a few days later, she kills herself.

Grover and his father have an uneasy truce thereafter. After
the funeral, his father tries to convince Grover that the death was
an accident. Grover knows better—"It was her trouble and that was
her way to get out of it" (81)—but he wisely realizes that his father
cannot accept the death at all, refusing to let his wife's things be
moved, withdrawing from life.

Life goes on for Grover, but when Betty Repking, a strange
woman never accepted by the town, taunts him about his mother's
suicide and says that it was a coward's way out, he retaliates by killing one of her pet turkeys. Strangely, he feels worse, not better. He
then seeks out the minister. He knows that he and his father must
share the grief, but a larger problem still remains. Is it true that "it's
the chief duty of every human being to endure life even when
they're sick and know they're going to die?" (116). Even the minister
can't help. Grover decides, "There's no sense in howling; it doesn't
do a bit of good. When something bad happens to you, like your
mother dying, you've got to go it alone, the way I've got it figured
out. You've got to use your gumption and common sense" (117).

He is wrong, of course. Through the help of his peers, Farrel
and Ellen Grae, the housekeeper Rose, and his uncle, Grover learns
to live again. And he realizes that, "after awhile things'll ease up"
(125). We even see his father smile, a tiny but significant indication
that he, too, can recover in time.

An exaggerated view of loyalty appears in Jane Yolen's *The
Stone Silenus*, a blend of mystery, the supernatural, and a realistic

look at unresolved grief. Unfortunately, the three do not merge successfully. Melissa Stanhold is obsessed with the memory of her father, Joshua, whom she idolizes. She remembers him almost as a god who could do no wrong; as a result, she is unhappy with her mother, who she feels is uncaring and whom she blames for the indiscretions of her father—including adultery. She is also furious at the suggestion that her father's drowning may have been suicide, not an accident.

A mysterious young man, Gabriel, approaches her one night on the beach, a favorite walking spot for Melissa and her father. He not only resembles a young Joshua Stanhold, but is also faunlike (most of her father's poetry dealt with fauns and satyrs). While she is drawn to this figure, she is also deeply afraid of him. She even wonders if he is not simply a figment of her imagination.

Complicating matters is her mother's romantic interest in Henry, her father's literary agent and lifetime friend. Once again, Melissa is appalled at her mother's "betrayal" of her father and her seemingly unfeeling nature.

Central to the novel is a sea gull that Melissa finds on the beach. Gabriel helps Melissa wash off the bird, and Melissa decides to try to nurse it back to health. The bird becomes increasingly menacing, however, and repulsive to her. Finally, at her mother's insistence, Melissa is taking the bird to a neighbor's to be cared for when she runs into Gabriel, who says he will take care of the bird. Later, they find the gull in front of their home, its eyes full of maggots.

In her confusion about Gabriel and her distress about the gull, she finally turns to her mother and Henry, the two people who knew her father best. In the painful conversation, she begins to realize that her father, while a good man, did have clay feet. For instance, it was not her mother but her father who didn't allow the children to have a pet. He was allergic to animal fur, but he could not admit any weakness. Thus Melissa has erroneously blamed her mother all along. His biggest fault, however, was his treatment of Melissa. "'Lissa, the one thing I can *never* forgive him for is that he tried to take you with him, to make you the perfect recorder of his invented image'" (94).

When they find the dead sea gull, Melissa realizes that Gabriel is very much real—and threatening. Although the police have been summoned to search the house and guard outside, Gabriel has hidden under her bed and tries to attack her. She is, of course, rescued, and we find that he is a mentally disturbed college student who once heard her father speak, wanted to be her father, and is convinced that he is possessed by Joshua's spirit.

The novel does a good job of showing the problems that arise when one glorifies the dead. Until Melissa can see her father as a real person, not a god, she cannot admit to his death or come to terms with it. The contrived plot, however, does not hold up.

Home Before Dark by Sue Ellen Bridges does a much better job. The book legitimately belongs in an adult category because of subject matter and characterization. Although the main character, Stella, is only fourteen, the insights into the adult characters as well make it more fitting for adult reading.

Stella's family, the Willises, are not common folk. Her father, James Earl, has left the family farm in North Carolina to join the army. Only sixteen years later does he return, having married Mae and fathered four children (one of whom has died). The couple have spent their entire lives as migrant workers, having no permanent home and living constantly on the road. Thus when James Earl decides to return to the family farm, Mae feels threatened. Unable to adjust to permanence and fearing that she will lose James Earl, she simply gives up. When lightning strikes and she is killed, the entire family believes that she wanted to die.

The story revolves around Stella, a restless, wise, sturdy creature whose dominant personality assures her a lovely and successful life. In the course of the book, however, she must give up some of her independence. Immediately, she is drawn to her Aunt Anne, the wife of James Earl's brother Newton, who now owns the family farm. Through Anne, Stella learns of the finer things in life. Not only does Anne buy her pretties, but she cultivates the softer side of Stella, guidance sadly missing from Stella's mother. We get glimpses into Anne, as well: her joy in her marriage, her yearning to be a perfect mother for the child she is carrying, her deep devotion to Stella.

In the meantime, Stella receives the attention of two boys: Toby, a neighbor, who struggles to be someone in the world, who loves her dearly, and who has worlds of decency, and Rodney, a repressed Mama's boy given everything material but nothing spiritual. Eventually, Rodney hires two goons to beat up Toby after he has seen Toby kiss Stella. At this point, Stella shows her spirit by refusing to have anything more to do with Rodney. And, after all, it is Toby who has given her the most comfort after Mae dies.

Caught up in all the excitement and yearnings of adolescence, lured by the prospects of the future, Stella is still torn. She refuses to be disloyal to her mother when James Earl decides to marry an older woman named Maggie. We see here the basic goodness of James, his need for a nurturer (unfulfilled by Mae), and his desire to provide a good home for his children. We also see the loving nature of Maggie, desperate to give all she has to James and his children.

When the rest of the family move into Maggie's elegant home, Stella refuses to leave her house, insisting that she can take care of herself. Gradually, however, she thaws, but clings to the only roots she has had.

> Loving never seemed to have anything to do with giving before. Daddy and Mama never had anything to give. None of us ever owned anything until we came back to Daddy's home and Newton gave us that little house. But, somehow, I felt like it has always been ours. That land out there belonged to us no matter what anyone said. Daddy was born to it, and I was born to Daddy; so the land and the house were mine (147).

Because not all parents are perfect, sometimes a child may not feel the normal bonds, the normal devotion. Three books, designed, naturally, for older children, do a splendid job of addressing this special problem.

In *You Never Lose* by Barbara Stretton, when Jim Halbert learns that his father, the high school football coach, is dying of cancer, he is distraught. Everyone loves Coach—everyone, that is, but Jim. Although Coach is a tyrant, although he never gives praise, he has earned the respect of all. Jim doesn't understand, for his father has been particularly hard on Jim, and no closeness exists. In the course of the novel, the reader learns to understand Coach even if he does not totally admire him. Coach is almost stereotypical in that he continues to strive for the glory that was once his as a hero both in high school and college. Jim is able to understand that glory twice in the book.

> What he'd felt the day he ran in the touchdown was love. He'd felt a group of people rise up and give him love. And whatever happened after that didn't really matter, not when he'd known that love.... And that's what it was all about—football. That's why guys got themselves bashed about like bull elephants—to feel the joy of the crowd's cheering. To feel the love. And once you've felt it—the way Jim did once, and the way his father must have over and over—well, there was no letting go. You had to chase after that love in game after game (170).

Now that he understands, he can accept his own love for his father.

Mr. Halbert must change also. Almost macho, he is not able to admit his sickness, insisting that he go on with his usual routine and not admitting the pain. When Jim overhears his father crying one night, he wants to help but realizes that his father cannot admit any "weakness." Eventually, Coach does begin to depend upon his wife, upon Jim and upon Jim's younger sister Liz. He agrees not to return to his job, but instead to travel with his wife.

Jim and Liz have also had other burdens to bear: the discomfort of being singled out at school as people to be pitied; their frustration over not being able to help each other or their mother in their private grief. And Jim is torn between two girls, one a real beauty whose priorities are superficial, the other a tough kid from West Virginia, bruised by life, cynical, but amazingly vulnerable.

The book has profanity in it and deals with sexual experiences; thus some parents might object. But it is beautiful in its portrayal of father-son difficulties and the pain of losing a loved one. Jim will not be like his fahter, holding everything in, but rather "holding on, the way he always did" (237).

Although *The Blanket World* by Honor Arundel is designated juvenile fiction, it requires a sophisticated reader because of the age of the first-person narrator (a twenty-year-old college student), her frequently abrasive personality, the emphasis on drinking, and the complicated insights offered.

Unlike the usual protagonists in books on death, Jan is not devastated by the impending and eventual death of her mother.

She is not even sure that she loves her mother. Nor is she close to the other members of her family, her two older sisters, Fanny and Beryl, wrapped up in their husbands and their children, and her older brother David, who has always been aloof and overly zealous in his responsibilities. While the absence of a father throughout most of her life and the age difference between her and her siblings may account for some of her difficulties, she is nevertheless an unappealing cold fish. She keeps her distance, views others with sarcasm and contempt, and holds superficial values. She turns her back on one boyfriend, Thomas, who is appalled when she will not even attend the funeral of her Aunt Agnes, a woman who had opened her home and her heart to Jan. When Jan returns home to see her dying mother, she feels primarily resentment. And once at home, she quarrels with her siblings, criticizes everything, and refuses to respond conventionally to her mother's death and the following rituals.

Jan does change somewhat. She realizes that she is not really grieving for her mother, but for the lack of any true relationship they might have had. She does come to know her brother David, begins to like him, and at the end of the book is willing to sacrifice part of her vacation to be with him and help with his children when David's wife, unable to overcome her grief, must be hospitalized. She renews her friendship with Thomas and begins to question the value of her relationship with her new boyfriend, who is charming and witty but basically self-centered and shallow.

The beauty of this book lies in its insightful view of the parent-child relationship. Frequently, children, wrapped in their own selfish concerns, do not really react to the death of a parent until much later simply because their understanding is so limited. Jan sees all parents as dull, boring, inflexible people simply to use and tolerate. She never really sees them as people with their own needs, their own problems, their own rights. Even Thomas, ordinarily compassionate and empathetic, complains of his mother and father. Both must learn to give, to accept and to understand.

Run Softly, Go Fast by Barbara Wersba is somewhat outdated since it covers the height of the "hippie" times. Yet, the conflicting emotions that the main character, David, goes through transcend the immediate setting. David is eighteen when the book begins, just after his father's funeral, when he feels compelled to write down his incredibly confused feelings. For several months before his father's death, the two have been completely alienated. David truly believes he hates his father, but memories continue to intrude and to baffle him.

David feels his entire life has been one of betrayal. As a child, he loved his father, Leo, cherishing the love and protection he always felt. As he grows older—and his father begins to realize the American Dream—David becomes cynical. Caught in the rat race of business and obsessed with succeeding, his father becomes corrupt in David's eyes. He turns his back on his former partner, engages in lies, and commits what David sees as the ultimate sin, having a string of affairs. No matter that much of what he does is to compensate for the bitter poverty of his childhood or to insure that David and his mother will have a better life. His father represents all that David deplores.

His father's brother, Uncle Ben, also has betrayed David. As an adolescent, David admired and loved his uncle for his other-worldliness, his love of beauty, his simplicity. When he tells Uncle Ben of his father's infidelity, however, Uncle Ben indicates that he does not want to hear or to become involved. David thinks,

> You knew what I was going to say and didn't want to hear it! Didn't want your peace disturbed, nor your loyalties split, nor your mind invaded by ugliness, nor your composure shattered by a knowledge you couldn't accept. . . . I saw you as you were . . . who pretended to be holy and pure and incorruptible because . . . *[you were] afraid of life* (52–3).

In a minor way, David also feels betrayed by his mother, who clings steadfastly to her husband, never admitting what he has become.

Many of the conflicts between David and his father are typical adolescent-parent disputes. Leo disapproves of the length of David's hair, his interests (poetry and painting), and most of all, his best friend, Rick. When Leo mistakenly accuses Rick of being gay, David finally has the courage to run away from home, living with a friend whom his father approves of, Marty, ironically a drug dealer.

David does his share of betraying as well. When Rick, a truly free spirit, returns from a visit with his father and reveals that he is going to enlist in the armed services, capitulating to his father's wishes, David turns his back on Rick, not even saying good-bye. Then when Rick is killed in Viet Nam, David cannot live with his guilt or his shame. For months, he becomes part of the drug scene in Greenwich Village. The author does a brilliant job in capturing the sadness and the sordidness of such a life.

David is blessedly rescued by Maggie, a girl who has also fled from home—for a better reason, her parents' alcoholism and abuse. Probably because of his father's extramarital affairs, David has not been able to have a relationship with a girl. Through Maggie's loving understanding, however, he is able to feel like a man. However, because the two are living together, his father refuses to meet her, once again rejecting what is important in his son's life. Maggie intuitively understands that until David comes to terms with his feelings over his father, he will not be entirely whole.

When his father becomes ill with terminal cancer and David visits him, the visit ends up in an argument. David vows never to return. But he does when the end is near, going day after day. "Now that it was too late, I was a faithful son. And I hated myself so much that the hate spilled out of me onto other people. . . . And finally onto Dad himself. Why? Because he was abandoning me" (196). Later, after his father's death, David realizes that although his father didn't come to David's art show, he did read the reviews, that he was proud of David. David realizes that he has told only

> . . .half the story. My half. Showing only one person's side. I read these pages and see Leo emerge as a kind of monster, when he was only . . . what? (202).

When he remembers, really remembers all the good about his father, he feels, "Crazy, crazy, to live your whole life with a person and not see him. And now it's too late. I'll never know who he was" (203).

> You did awful things to me, hurt me so badly. . . .but your father did awful things to you, and his father did the same to him. The same mistakes over and over, no one learning from the past. . . . I wanted a father in my image . . . and you wanted a son in yours . . . so we missed each other at every crossroad. . . .I keep wishing you were alive so we could start over. . . . The

only important thing is that you lived on this earth for a while and were my father, and that I came from you, and that my children will come from me. A long line of people, blind to one another, hurting one another . . . but surviving. . . . And if it's true – that living is the thing, no matter how painful – then I can thank you for my life, the gift of it. . . . I don't hate you anymore, Leo (204–5).

Finally, three books stress that no matter how bad the blow a parent's death delivers, life goes on.

In *The Kenton Years* by Ruth Wallace-Brodeur, nine-year-old Mandy McPherson cannot adjust to her father's death. After he is killed on the street by a drunk driver, Mandy has incredible difficulties. Finally, she refuses even to go to school. To remedy the situation, Mrs. McPherson plans a summer vacation in Vermont, where she herself summered as a child.

The author does suggest that Mandy does not quickly forget her father. Unfortunately, those incidents dealing with him occur frequently and seem forced. For instance, both Mandy and her mother seem uninterested in Christmas, the first since Mr. McPherson's death, but immediately plunge into the festivities. When Mandy learns to ski and enters with great zeal into practice for the winter races, her mother is concerned. It is hinted that qualifying for the races will somehow rid her of the "strange tyrant" (81). But how her success is connected with her grief over her father is unclear. By the end of the book, all conflicts have been resolved. She builds a plaque in memory of her father, and she and her mother go on with their lives. The book does stress the joys of living, but it does a superficial job of treating grief and its ramifications.

Ganesh by Malcolm J. Bosse does a better job in emphasizing the positive. It is well worth reading even if the explanation of death relies on the interpretation of a different culture and a different religion. Jeffrey has lived with his father in India nearly all his fourteen years, hence his nickname of Ganesh after a Hindu god. After spending several years there as a social worker, his father rejects his former life and embraces Hinduism. Jeffrey's mother died when he was nine. Now his father is ill and dies within a few weeks.

Steeped in the religious traditions of India, Jeffrey goes through the customary rituals, including the cremation of his father (it is

Jeffrey who lights the blaze). Unsure that he still believes (the gods seem to have deserted him), Jeffrey still follows the traditions. Having promised his father that he will return to America after his father's death, and knowing that he will be considered a stranger in his village, he refuses to leave India without disposing of his father's ashes in the same sacred river where he and his father said farewell to Jeffrey's mother. At this point, he feels a union with his mother, his father, the world at large: "'We are here. We are everywhere.' He followed the soaring, pulsing rhythm of another flock of birds rising from the riverbank. Everywhere. 'We are here and everywhere'" (62).

In the second section of the book, Jeffrey must learn to adjust to his new home in the Midwest with his Aunt Betty. While the two of them like each other immediately and form a lasting relationship, his adjustments are difficult. Americans do not understand his vegetarianism, his habits like belching in public, his reliance on meditation.

As time goes on, he does make friends. Eventually, he and several of his classmates join in an Indian ritual of fasting as nonviolent resistance to the government's confiscating his aunt's home to put in a new highway. The people around Jeffrey are beginning to understand and appreciate the cultural values that help govern his life.

While this second half of the book appears to have little to do with death, the house that Jeffrey and his aunt are fighting for reveals a major insight. Because the home was built by Jeffrey's great-grandfather, it holds for him the spirit of all his ancestors, "a place of shelter, a home of memory" (185). Jeffrey will continue to draw upon both the spirit of his father and the spirit of his forefathers.

The most affirmative of all is *The Big Wave* by Pearl Buck. This lovely little book reminds one of a folk tale in its beauty and simplicity. Kino, whose family lives on a farm, and Jiya, whose family fish and thus live by the sea, are best of friends. The Japanese have great respect for the sea, knowing its power to destroy; in fact, their houses have no windows on the sides facing the water. While Kino enjoys the beauty of the sea and has a wonderful time swimming, one day he feels its power, its depth, and is afraid. His father tells him that land can be dangerous, too, and reminds him of the nearby volcano:

Ocean is there and volcano is there. It is true that on any day ocean may rise into storm and volcano may burst into flame. We must accept this fact, but without fear. We must say, "Someday I shall die, and does it matter whether it is by the ocean or volcano, or whether I grow old and weak?" (16).

Later, his father advises him,

> "There are times when the gods leave man to take care of himself.... They test us, to see how able we are to save ourselves.... Fear alone makes man weak. If you are afraid, your hands tremble, your feet falter, and your brain cannot tell hands and feet what to do" (21).

Soon they are all to meet that test. When the volcano erupts, the disturbance underground causes a tidal wave that wipes out the entire fishing village on the shore. Only a few of the children escape. Reluctantly, Jiya has left his family to seek refuge with Kino's family. Buck treats his grief and mourning with depth and simplicity. Above all, it is Kino's father's wisdom that helps all endure. He is totally understanding of the tears Kino sheds over the loss his friend has sustained and later over the possibility that Jiya may leave to live with a wealthy old man who has offered to adopt him. He also understands that Jiya needs time, but that he will triumph over grief:

> "Yes, he will be happy someday ... for life is always stronger than death.... He will cry and cry and we must let him cry.... He will sit sad and quiet. We must allow him to be sad and we must not make him speak.... Then one day he will be hungry ... all the time his body will be renewing itself. His blood flowing in his veins, his growing bones, his mind beginning to think again, will make him live" (28–9).

Kino's father is correct. Finally, Jiya is able to adjust, helped by the love and friendship of Kino's mother, father, and little sister Setsu. The years pass, and when Jiya is a young man, he asks for Setsu's hand in marriage and determines to become a fisherman, to erect a new home on the old site on the beach. Although some question his decision, again it is Kino's father who sums up the role of death in life: He has explained to Kino that just as babies resist being born,—"'You wanted to stay just where you were in the warm, dark house of the unborn'"—so do people resist dying: "'But someday you will wonder why you were afraid, even as today you wonder why you feared to be born'" (37). He expresses his wonderful philosophy:

> "To live in the presence of death makes us brave and strong. . . . To die a little later or a little sooner does not matter. . . . We love life because we live in danger. We do not fear death because we understand that life and death are necessary to each other" (37).

V. One's Own Death

Time held me green and dying
Though I sang in my chains like the sea.

"Fern Hill"
Dylan Thomas

From the minute a child is born, he is, indeed, "green and dying." Early experiences, such as peek-a-boo, begin to expose him to
separation. Likewise, folklore subtly introduces the child to mortality. Since children before the age of five seldom accept death as permanent and those five to ten generally do not see themselves as
mortal, books about one's own death are scarce for children under
ten—with good reason. In general, such books would be inappropriate. Children in the early elementary grades find particularly
difficult and traumatic a violent death of a classmate, forcing them
too early to realize their own vulnerability. Nevertheless, a few
books for this age group deserve mention. For instance, in *The
Beaver Who Wouldn't Die*, a mildly amusing book by M.G. De
Bruyn, a beaver named Cyrus attends the funeral of his Uncle
Abner and vows that he himself will never die. After a few years
pass, a pink fairy grants him a wish if he will spare a magic tree.
When he wishes never to die, she calls him a "foolish beaver" and
warns him that he will not be happy. But he persists, and his wish
is granted. As the years go by, he grows old but never weak or sick.
As a result of his great age, the other beavers consider him wise and
consult him frequently. Soon, all the problems "started to sound
the same." And, because beavers never stop growing, after a thousand years he is so large that he must go live by himself in a huge
cave on a huge lake where he ekes out a lonely existence. Finally,
he has a nightmare that he grows so big, the world will not support

137

him so that he must float in space forever. He cries out, "'I wish I had never been born! . . . I wish I were dead!'" Suddenly, he is once more in the arms of his mother, small again. She tells him, "'This is not the end. You have yet to begin.'"

The book does show that endless life would indeed probably get boring and tedious. The ending is unclear, however. Has the entire experience been a dream? Such interpretation is not likely, since Cyprus becomes an adult before his wish is granted. Then has he gone to an afterlife? If so, the book is misleading in that heaven is a literal place offering eternal life.

Another book that may come under fire because it deals with a literal interpretation of heaven is *Jake and Honeybunch Go to Heaven* by Margot Zemach. When the two main characters die and reach heaven, they find people in ordinary clothes engaging in ordinary activities, and God is personified as a tall man, with a mustache, wearing a white suit. Nevertheless, because the story, based on a black folk tale, is so charming, it may be appropriate.

Jake has a crazy mule named Honeybunch, who is "contrary"— the first illustration shows an accident, with Honeybunch draped over the hood of an automobile and Jake flailing around in the cart that Honeybunch is pulling. Jake always would say, "'This misbegotten mule will be the death of me someday!'" And so his prediction comes to pass when Honeybunch meets with a freight train.

When Jake gets to the Pearly Gates and finds no one there, he simply enters. Spying wings that are hanging up to dry, he confiscates two of them and begins to fly through heaven. Unfortunately, because both are left wings, he creates havoc. God intervenes, sending him outside the Pearly Gates. Honeybunch approaches and, spying the Great Green Pastures, plunges through the gates. Not surprisingly, Honeybunch creates even more chaos. Defeated, God agrees to let Jake back in so that he can control his mule. For eternity, they are assigned the job of hanging out the moon and the stars each night. Most readers will enjoy the pure fun of the book, and certainly the tale makes death less fearsome.

A very popular book for young children is *The Fall of Freddie the Leaf* by Leo Buscaglia. Although somewhat didactic (the insights leave little to the imagination), this book does point out that death is a natural part of life and does stress that one must make use of his life. Freddie the leaf lives on a large branch near the top of a tree. Surrounded by hundreds of other leaves, Freddie realizes that no two are alike. Freddie's best friend, Daniel, is both the largest and the wisest of all the leaves. Through Daniel, Freddie learns not only about his environment but about the meaning of life and death. For instance, Daniel explains that every living thing has a purpose: One of their purposes as leaves is to provide shade for the people who come to the park.

When October comes, the weather cools, and the winds become violent, Daniel explains about death: "'Everything dies. No matter how big or small, how weak or strong. We first do our job. We experience the sun and the moon, the wind and the rain. We learn to dance and to laugh. Then we die.'" When Freddie admits that he is afraid, Daniel comforts him: "'We all fear what we don't know, Freddie. It's natural ... you were not afraid when Spring became Summer. You were not afraid when Summer became Fall. They were natural changes. Why should you be afraid of the season of death?'" Daniel further explains that while individuals die, life itself will go on. Freddie is still not appeased: "'Then what has been the reason for all of this? ... Why were we here at all if we only have to fall and die?'" Daniel reiterates all the joys they have experienced and concludes, "'Isn't that enough?'"

Soon, Daniel dies, leaving Freddie all alone. During the first snowfall, the winds blow Freddie from his branch. "It didn't hurt at all. He felt himself float quietly, gently and softly downward." He realizes that "he had been a part of life and it made him proud." Further, Freddie has never realized that "what appeared to be his useless dried self would join with the water and serve to make the tree stronger. Most of all, he did not know that there, asleep in the tree and the ground, were already plans for new leaves in the Spring." In the last photograph, showing a tree in bud with a bird perched on a branch, are the words, "The Beginning." Through the simple tale and through the beautiful photographs of nature in all of its seasons, the book stresses both death as a natural part of life and the cyclical nature of existence.

Finally, *All the Living* by Claudia Mills gently and humorously introduces death to fourth and fifth graders. Karla is "into" death. As she and her family travel from New Jersey to Maine to vacation at the cabin left to them by Great-uncle James, Karla is frantic because James died in the cabin. On their way, she has counted thirteen animals dead on the road. She looks at the dead trees and feels sad. When she eats an egg, she thinks of its former potential as a chicken. Not surprisingly, after she sees a fish head, she adamantly refuses to eat any meat, fish, or fowl. Her preoccupation with death is actually amusing and becomes hysterical when she even feels reluctant to eat a piece of fudge. Underneath, of course, her obsession is a real problem with a real basis.

For in a science project, she and a classmate had taken two tiny caterpillars and cared for them as they spun chrysalises through the winter and watched them emerge from their cases. Unfortunately, as Karla laid her butterfly on the ground to ready itself for flight, a classmate, Danny Pines, deliberately crushed the butterfly under his feet. Although Karla understands that Danny's parents were going through a divorce and that he was emotionally disturbed, she cannot accept that people can kill anything.

The problem comes to a head when her brother Jamie catches a four-pound bass. Jamie has had a hard life because of his father. Jamie is not athletic; he much prefers to read. As a result, he is a bitter disappointment to his father, who doesn't bother to hide his scorn for his son. No matter what Jamie endeavors, he can never satisfy his father. Their mother is a lovely person, but she is a conciliator, never really interfering and thus perpetuating the problem. When Karla sees the dead fish, she calls her brother a murderer— "And, like their father used to do, Karla looked away" (105).

The mother finally takes a stand, insisting that the children go to the lake and resolve their differences. As they are rowing in the middle of the lake, a sudden storm hits, Karla falls overboard, and Jamie rescues her. In the hospital, Karla is finally able to gain some perspective on life and death. Immediately, eating her delicious breakfast, she recognizes the joy of being alive. Later, Mrs. Whalen, an elderly acquaintance of the family, tells Karla: "'Living's scary, too. . . . It's scary and it's wonderful and you might as well do it while you can'" (125). This belief is reaffirmed in a passage from Ecclesiastes that Karla reads: "'And I commend enjoyment, for man has no good thing under the sun but to eat and drink, and enjoy himself'" (124). Finally, in recognizing that she, too, must die, Karla also realizes that "joined with all the living, there was hope . . . (126).

One other book deserves mention. *The Story of Ick* by Fred Gwynne seeks to raise the consciousness of the very young to the incredible destruction pollution may bring to our planet. The book is both charming and chilling. As a little boy searches the beach to find something to play with, he finds only sticky, sharp or smelly objects. Suddenly, he discovers an "icky-looking" thing. "Ick was sticky but not too sticky, sharp, but not too sharp, and smelly, but not too smelly." When the boy makes a scary face, Ick runs down the beach, the boy chasing him and finally catching him. Now it is Ick who makes a scary face, chasing the boy, catching him, and taking him to Ick's mother and father. Ick's parents make Ick return the boy to the beach—"'There are hardly any little boys on the beach anymore. Maybe if you put him back—some more will grow.'" Ick cries as he lets the child go, but "from that day on—Ick could never find another little boy to play with."

On one level, the reader will find the book suspenseful, and many can relate to the loneliness both Ick and the boy feel, the need they experience for a friend. On a deeper level, the book addresses the problems of pollution, the smelly, sharp, sticky refuse that may indeed take over the world, making it uninhabitable.

Fortunately, a number of books exist for parents with terminally ill children. Unfortunately, these books do not offer immediate comfort for the child who is dying. Several books, most of them worthwhile, deal with the impending death of the protagonist because of illness.

The least successful book is *This Day Is Mine* by Jane Miner. Since the protagonist is sixteen, the picture-book format is hardly appropriate. And the didacticism is stifling. Nevertheless, it is better than nothing. Cheryl has been in the hospital for two weeks. Even though she is to go home, she is still depressed and frequently cries. She doesn't understand what is wrong with her, and she fears the worst. Not helping matters any are her parents, who, in a move to protect her, avoid telling her the truth. Their manners, however, seem strained and contribute to her anxiety. Finally, through the encouragment of the medical staff, her mother agrees to let Cheryl talk to the doctor, Dr. Adams, a kind, professional woman. Dr. Adams tells Cheryl that she has leukemia, but that some people with leukemia live for three years, more than half live five years, and many more than ten. "'Think of it this way. Your job is to stay alive today, so you can be cured tomorrow. We've learned so much, Cheryl. We can learn a lot more'" (25).

Much anger follows. At first, she turns the anger toward her parents, somewhat legitimately because they have lied to her. Much, of course, is aimed at the "unfairness" of the world. Finally, a fight erupts with much shouting and accusations. When Cheryl finds that weekly she will have to go into the hospital for tests, she determines to run away.

On her way to her Aunt Marsha's in the city, requiring a subway trip in the middle of the night, she is accosted by a man. As she flees from him, she falls and cuts her knee. Finally arriving exhausted at her aunt's, she becomes terrified because her knee is bleeding. She knows that with her condition, any bleeding becomes dangerous. Suddenly she realizes that she *wants* to live as long as she can, and she gladly goes to the hospital.

Once there, she learns another lesson. When she is asked by a nurse to befriend a younger child who also has leukemia, Cheryl is reluctant but agrees. The courage and the optimism of the child give her new spirit. She resolves to go back to school and to count her blessings, including parents who love her.

May I Cross You Golden River? by Paige Dixon is so real to life, one has difficulty remembering that the main character, Jordan Phillips, is fictional. A college freshman, a natural athlete with a promising life ahead of him, Jordan develops Lou Gehrig's disease, which produces atrophy and weakening of the muscles and leads, usually quickly, to death. In depth, we learn of Jordan's reactions to his illness and impending death, the reactions of his family, and the ways in which they all learn to cope and to accept. Jordan goes through the initial stages of bargaining—perhaps the diagnosis is wrong. He becomes angry at his body—why is it failing him in this way? He is ashamed of his loss of strength and his inability to handle normal tasks. He is afraid of the reactions of others, particularly his girlfriend, who he knows will not be able to accept his fate. And of course, he is depressed much of the time. He also feels guilt that he is causing so much suffering for his family, who sacrifice both time and money to insure that his last months on earth are as happy as possible.

The family is marvelous. They manage to provide Jordan with insight and with normalcy. For instance, they tell him, "'The

sovereignty of sorrow doesn't release a person from human obligation'" (110). And he is included in a brother's wedding and his
nephew's christening.

Most importantly, Jordan uses his time wisely. He remains close
to his family, he becomes even closer to his younger brother Skip-
per, he renews his interest in painting, and he reaches out to others,
a couple whose farmhouse he stops at when his car won't start and
an old mountaineer he meets on a weekend trip. When Jordan dies,
his entire family is there to comfort him, and he embraces death
peacefully: "He let his head fall sideways on the pillow. He was too
tired to talk anymore" (262).

Two books, both written by a parent, reveal the true story of
a child who has died of leukemia. The title of *Death Be Not Proud,
A Memoir* by John Gunther, a tribute to the author's son who died
at age seventeen, comes from a John Donne sonnet, an appropriate
honor to Johnny Gunther, who "beat" death by not giving into it,
by maintaining his optimism, his patience, and his courage.
Because of the time period, the forties, the doctors and Johnny's
parents treated the illness not as people would today; they did not
discuss his upcoming death openly; indeed, they frequently lied to
him, for instance, putting him in the hospital for a seven-hour
operation without revealing the reason for the operation.

In addition, the book is aimed more at parents than children.
The author dwells continually on the various medical symptoms,
treatments, theories and procedures. While such preoccupation is
typical of both the terminally ill and their loved ones, some children
might find these specifics boring. Another problem lies in distance.
Had Gunther waited more than than two years to write this
memoir, more perspective might have evolved. Nevertheless, the
book does reveal three crucial insights to the child reader.

Although Johnny is to die (and the parents realize after his
death that he has known the seriousness of his condition all along),
all three make the most of his time. Frequently, he complains of
wasting time, and he continues to set new goals, meeting many of
them before his death. Further, because the father in particular has
saved all of his son's correspondence—letters and journals—and
remembers in poignant detail even small, insignificant remarks,
jokes, gestures, a terminally ill reader will realize how special he will
always be to those who love him.

Finally, Gunther sums up his view of death:

> ...his spirit, and only his spirit, that kept him invincibly alive
> against such dreadful obstacles for so long—this is the central
> pith and substance of what I am trying to write, as a mournful
> tribute not only to Johnny but to the power, the wealth, the un-
> conquerable beauty of the human spirit, will and soul (193).

And Johnny's mother writes that the wish that she had loved
Johnny more simply means

> ...loving life more, being more aware of life, of one's fellow
> human beings, of the earth.... Obliterating, in a curious but
> real way, the ideals of evil and hate and enemy ... caring more
> and more about other people ... (260).

Doris Lund in *Eric* has written her personal account of the battle her son Eric had with leukemia and his eventual death. Unlike
Gunther in *Death Be Not Proud*, Mrs. Lund gives not only her reactions but is able to give insight into Eric's feelings as well. Much of
the book, of course, covers the medical side—the symptoms, the
treatments, the research. During each remission of the illness, the
reader rejoices with the family. During each crisis, the reader suffers
with them.

We do come to appreciate the marvelous courage and spirit of
Eric, who refuses to let others control him, to give in to the disease,
to stop living life to its fullest. The first lesson his mother learns as
she worriedly watches him go off to a football game on a bitterly
cold day is that

> Now might be all he would ever have. He had to live his life.
> And living meant running risks. There was no way to wrap him
> in cotton. He had to run free to be a whole man. I wanted that.
> I discovered I wanted it more than my own peace of mind or my
> need to mother him and be sure I'd done all I could (31).

Unfortunately, this decision—to let Eric be in control—causes
her undue agony in the ensuing years. Eric will not allow her to express her sorrow (indeed, one evening she stuffs a towel in her
mouth to stifle her cries), she must not consult with his doctors, he

even restricts her visits when he is in the hospital. While the reader admires her courage, her willingness to suffer to make her child happy, he also sees that everyone involved must express grief. For her to deny her own feelings is a terrible sacrifice, one that Eric really did not have the right to expect. In this respect, Mrs. Lund is far too hard on herself. The results are also hard on the entire family because of the tension involved.

Another question the book asks but never resolves is the quality of life. After one long, agonizing bout of illness, one wonders if Eric should not have been better to give in, to die, and thus to spare himself and the family from such torture. Yet good days remain for him. Only at the end do they finally decide that they will not allow resuscitation.

Throughout, the most positive aspect of the book is the zest for life that all exhibit, not only Eric but the other patients, all terminally ill, whom he meets in his many hospital stays. Likewise, the medical staff are marvelous, as are the patients' families and others as well—for instance, the many strangers who routinely give blood. In fact, the book ends as Eric's father returns to the blood bank. In keeping others alive, the Lunds hope that one day they will see a cure for leukemia and can claim their part as a victory for Eric.

Hang Tough, Paul Mather by Alfred Slote is particularly significant because its emphasis on sports may attract male readers, perhaps otherwise reluctant to read of death. Paul Mather has leukemia. We see all the symptoms and side effects: the danger of being hit or cut, the nausea, burning and itching that come from the medication, the sudden, inexplicable remissions, the overall weakness. Likewise, we see how others treat him: his father quickly supportive, his mother protective and anxious, his younger brother Punk uncomfortable but loving. Also helping Paul are Brophie, "one tough nurse," and Dr. Kinsella, not only a skilled physician but also a friend.

Sustaining Paul through his ordeal are his love of and skill in baseball. The family having moved to Michigan to be near Dr. Kinsella, Paul, a consummate pitcher, forges his father's name to a Little League form and plays his first game. In the bottom of the second inning, Paul collides with the first baseman and needs immediate hospitalization. Although he is considerably worse, considerably weaker, he finally bullies the doctor and his family into letting him out of the hospital a month later for one day to watch his team battle for a place in the play-offs. During the game, Paul is able to help, even from his wheelchair, and the team wins.

While his family are certainly supportive, Paul is able to discuss his disease and his probable death only with Tom Kinsella. Indeed, he is able to name his disease out loud only to Tom. One day, they have an insightful talk about death itself. Paul realizes:

> [I] . . . had death inside me. I could feel it sometimes hard as a rock and sometimes soft and running crazy through my veins. I knew it firsthand. . . . "Yes . . . I'm scared. Even when I'm so nauseous I wish I were dead, I'm still scared of dying" (123).

Yet hope exists. When Paul tells his doctor that leukemia has no cure, Tom tells him, "'Some day there will be a cure for leukemia. Good people all over the world, the best scientists, are working day and night to discover a cure'" (45), emphasizing that the terminally ill must never give up hope. And the book ends indeterminately: "We're hanging tough. It's not easy. There's pain, and Tom says lots more to come. But Tom also says time is on my side. Time and medicine and research and my own battling instincts. If anyone can make it, he says, I can" (156). The will to live is invaluable.

Two books show young readers that not only illness and disease may strike, but danger as well. Although *Soldier and Me* by David Line deals only tangentially with one's own mortality, it is certainly worth reading. When fourteen-year-old Woolcott rescues a young Hungarian boy from the harassment of a street gang, Szolda, or Soldier as Woolcott calls him, becomes his faithful shadow. Because Soldier's English is halting, because he is skinny and odd, Woolcott resents his adoration; at the same time, he feels sorry for him. Soon, however, Soldier is to involve him in far more difficult situations.

At the library, Soldier has overheard two men plot the death of an old crippled man. At first reluctant, Woolcott is soon drawn into an intricate series of spying, witnessing a murder, being rebuffed by the police, and finally escaping from a group of cutthroats. The chase itself is marvelous, involving much hardship, daring, close escapes, and suprisingly, much humor.

When the men finally capture Woolcott and Soldier, both boys realize they are to be killed. At first, both cry. Then Woolcott regrets never seeing his mother or his home again. Then he becomes remote. "I knew nothing was ever going to frighten me again" (171). The two, of course, are rescued and in the nature of children bounce back again, but Woolcott will never take life for granted again.

Anyone familiar with Elsa the lioness in *Born Free* will find *In The Jaws of Death* by Judith Stone of interest since it takes place in the same compound, Hora Camp, a home for orphaned lions. George Adamson, the founder of the camp, is a character in this book as well. The story belongs to Tony Fitzjohn, however, and his favorite orphaned lion, Freddie, whom the author treats appealingly but without undue sentimentality. We never lose sight of the fact that Freddie is a wild animal.

The major focus of the book is an attack on Tony by a full-grown lion who has been poisoned. Tony is quite literally in the jaws of death as the beast repeatedly attacks him. It is Freddie who tries to protect Tony and who finally is able to rouse the attention of the others at camp. They drive off the lion, nurse Tony through the night, and arrange for air transport to Nairobi. Tony does recover and does return to his work with the lions.

The author does not deal much with the subject of death itself. During the attack, Tony assumes that he will die—"he couldn't fight 400 pounds of lion" (19), and the people at camp are too far removed to help. He thinks of his girlfriend and his life in Africa. He even wonders who will take over his job and is sad that he won't be around to see Freddie grow into a lion. The message here, while subtle, is twofold: if one has lived a satisfying life, he can accept his own death; and life is, indeed, fraught with peril.

Most children in the United States will escape serious injury or illness. Yet they all face a terrifying possibility—death by war.

> Perhaps in no other era have the gods played such cruel games with youth. While this present generation in America can be said to be the first death-free generation in the world [death-free meaning the lowest incidence of death in young people in this country ever], the prospect of sudden mass extermination by a nuclear attack hangs threateningly over their heads. Contempt for authority and impatience with the older generation reflect their hostile attitude toward this bittersweet inheritance (Fulton 37).

Are young people's fears of nuclear war exaggerated? Hardly. Susan Becker cites numerous studies showing that children eight to ten begin to worry about war; they "'. . . begin to see that they and their family, even their city and country, are small parts of a complex universe, subject to larger forces'" (88). And the fears are there, even if the children don't express them:

> If a threat is too oppressive to live with, [it] may be denied. . . . Our children, who take many of their cues from the adults in their environment, have come to feel that this is not a topic for conversation (88).

James Mackey agrees:

> . . . contemporary children feel that there is no escape from the inevitability of destruction, and they do not expect to reach adulthood. . . . They come to feel that only the present has importance. The past is meaningless, and the future impossible to prepare for because it can disappear at the whim of a distant politician (127-8).

As a result, several enlightened school systems have included in their curricula units on war to help children cope with these fears, to let them know others share these fears, and to work on "conflict resolution, reconciliation, means of avoiding war, or ways of sustaining international goodwill" (Mackey 127). Becker cites a poem about war written by a high school student that sums up the need with its final statement that "knowing may save us" (89).

Children's books about war thus play a significant role. Mackey explains:

> Younger children are interested in the concrete aspects of war such as guns, tanks, and airplanes. As they near adolescence, children begin to recognize some of the actions and consequences of war. Gradually they lose some of their concern with the machinery of war and begin to concentrate more on the reality of men fighting, killing, and dying (127).

Thus books on war aimed at younger children attempt to introduce to them the harsh reality of war.

One Sad Day by Bernice Kohn, for instance, although weakened by unimaginative drawings and a tendency toward didacticism, nevertheless has a valid message. The Spots are a rural people, enjoying the beauty and peacefulness of nature. The Stripes are an urban people, enjoying the comforts of technology and culture. One day, the Stripes decide to make war on the Spots, simply because their culture is different. In the end, *all* the people are gone.

> Now the war is over and it is quiet everywhere. . . . Of all that was once happy and beautiful there is now nothing left. For war kills.

Barbara Emberley in *Drummer Hoff* has taken what is presumably a cumulative nursery rhyme and made it into an antiwar statement. As the action progresses, a different ranking member of the army makes his contribution to the firing of a cannon, e.g. "Sergeant Chowder brought the powder." Most children love cumulative stories, and the illustrations are full of bright color and amusing detail. At the bottom of each page is a border of grass and flowers. However, when Drummer Hoff fires the cannon, the full-page spread, with jarring colors of orange, hot pink, vivid turquoise, and deep purple, jarring lines, and in bright yellow letters KAHBAHBLOOM, is terrifying. The last picture shows the cannon, covered with flowers. Insects are hovering about, birds have built a nest there and are feeding their young, and a spider has spun a web, suggesting that nature will reclaim the earth, man having wiped himself from it.

In *Bang, Bang, You're Dead* by Louise Fitzhugh and Sandra Scoppettone, James, Timothy, Stanley, and Bert choose up sides and play war. Trying to take over the same hill, they shout, "Bang, bang, you're dead," and all fall down. Immediately, they get up and go for ice cream. One day, however, when they meet to play war, a gang of older boys meet them and challenge them to a battle the next day to determine who "owns" the hill. James, Timothy, Stanley, and Bert have a strategy meeting and vow to fight "'to the end'" (21). We see only an illustration of the actual battle; the boys, looking mean and menacing, hurl rocks at each other. At the end, "There were screams, yells, blood, and pain. It was awful" (26–7). Timothy says, "'This isn't any fun. . . . Why did we do it'" (28), and

James says, "'Nobody won'" (29). Unbelievably, the older boys agree to meet the next day, not to play "real war," but "bang, bang, you're dead" war.

The best of these books for younger children is Dr. Seuss's *The Butter Battle Book*. The book is typical Dr. Seuss, with zany characters, lilting rhymes, catchy alliteration. But the message is totally serious. The Yooks, who eat their bread with the buttered side up, have for centuries been fighting the Zooks, who eat their bread with the buttered side down. Separated by a wall that gets higher and higher, each side continues to develop more effective weapons until each side has a Big-Boy Boomeroo.

The wall, of course, is symbolic of the barriers men have created throughout history to preserve cultural "purity" and national pride; and the differences men choose to hate each other for have traditionally been nearly as silly as the way one eats his bread and butter. The ridiculous names of the weapons—a Nick-Berry Switch, a Triple-Sling Jigger, a Jigger-Rock Snatchem, a Kick-a-Poo Kid with Poo-a-Doo Powder, an Eight-Nozzled, Elephant-toted Boom-Blitz, an Utterly Sputter, a Blue-Gooer—barely disguise the development of weapons from sticks, sling shots and stones to bigger and more powerful guns, fighter planes, and chemical warfare. The Big-Boy Boomeroo, of course, is the bomb. The book ends as we wait to see whether the Yooks or the Zooks will drop it first. "'Be patient,' said Grandpa. 'We'll see. We will see....'"

Books of this ilk for older children are more realistic, more brutal, and thus more terrifying. War dominates *Dawn of Fear* by Susan Cooper, a sophisticated book on three different levels. As the book begins, the main character Derek, his two friends, Geoff and Peter, and their families, living twenty miles from London during the Second World War, must face air raids almost daily. The boys not only accept these raids as routine, they do not feel the effects of rationing as their parents do, nor do they experience the fear, anxiety, and indecision of their parents; in fact, the air raids bring excitement to their lives. They are thrilled with the drama and are caught up with the glory they mistakenly attach to the military. They know all the different types of aircraft and are impressed by an older neighbor, Tom, who at sixteen has enlisted in the Merchant Navy. At the same time, on another level, they are "playing war." In a ditch, the beginning of an excavation for an apartment house left uncompleted because of the war, they are constructing a camp, complete with weapons (a toy gun and hand-fashioned darts for a blow gun made out of discarded pipe), a secret hiding place for their treasures, and proper concealment (shrubs for camouflage and a wall—or "battlements").

The true meaning and horror of war come through to Derek quickly. His parents are concerned about his innocence, yet wish to protect him. "'Even to Derry it doesn't mean much. Just a great game, like cowboys and Indians. It's hard—you have to teach them to be careful, yet you don't want to teach them to be afraid'" (29). One night, however, when Derek is loitering as usual on the family's way to the bomb shelter in the backyard, his father grabs him and shoves him into the shelter. Suddenly, Derek is terrified.

> Like anybody else, he knew what it was like to be scared by things like the snapping of a large dog, by bigger boys chasing him at school, by being alone in the dark. But the guns and the bombs and the swooping planes, they were different. Nothing about them had ever really bothered him before—not, at any rate, until that fierce moment this evening, with the strange urgent note in his father's voice and the violence with which he had pulled him down (60).

At this point in the novel, the treatment of war on the final level emerges. Already beginning to realize the horror of war, Derek discovers its true meaning. Earlier, he and his friends have rescued a stray cat from the clutches of a gang of toughs from a nearby neighborhood. In retaliation, the gang, led by David Wiggs and his older brother Johnny, destroy the boys' camp, including Derek's darts and Geoff's prize collection of birds' eggs, take Peter's gun, and leave the corpse of the drowned kitten rescued earlier. After burying the cat, the boys, with Tom's aid, decide to strike back, ambushing the gang and pummeling them with mud balls. Suddenly, however, the rather routine fight takes on a different nature. Tom and Johnny square off and begin to fight, not as children, but as men:

> Not like their own kind of fighting at all, but something much

> older and bigger and with emotions behind it of a kind they did
> not know. . . . He could hardly bear to look at their faces, each
> now and then visible for a flaring second out of the whirl of
> angry limbs or the wary, watchful circling that punctuated the
> scuffling bursts. . . . Their faces had changed utterly; they were
> twisted up in some vast adult emotion as if they were fighting
> some fight that was not about themselves only, but about far
> bigger things. There was the sneer of real hatred on the faces . . .
> almost as if the whole world had suddenly divided into two and
> the two halves were flinging themselves one against the other
> (133–6).

The fight ends only because of the sirens signaling yet another air raid and forcing all the boys to speed home.

Derek's jolt into reality is compounded when he learns the next morning that his beloved friend Peter and his family have been killed by a bomb.

> The misery and fright were growing inside him like a great swell-
> ing balloon. Yesterday the world had begun going badly wrong,
> but it was to have been better again when today came; the bits
> of nightmare could have been forgotten. But instead today had
> brought a change that would need more than forgetting. His
> world had stopped, and the world he would live in from now
> on would be a different world (149).

The unreal quality of the day continues for Derek until he begs and is allowed to go see what remains of Peter's house. As Derek stares at the devastation, he glimpses the one thing that ". . . told him this unimaginable chaotic ruin had indeed once been the Hutchins house—the front gate." It is at this moment that he realizes fully what war means; it is no longer a game to him. When David Wiggs, his enemy, approaches and hands Peter's gun to Derek, his grief finally surfaces. He shoves David aside, begins to sob, and runs blindly to the ditch to bury the gun alongside the cat killed through cruelty and ignorance. Only when he has paid this tribute to his friend do his sobs cease.

> . . . he could breathe without gasping, and under the cold sun-

shine of the April day he sat down in the ruin of the camp, and put his head on his knees, and cried (157).

In Spite of All Terror by Hester Burton is also a World War II adventure. While fictional, it is based on actual events, giving it immediacy. The protagonist, Liz Hawtin, feels displaced. Having lost her father three years earlier, she faces many conflicts in her fifteenth year. She is forced to live with her uncle's family. Not only do they constantly remind her that her father was a waste (he was a committed Communist), but her Aunt Ag is a bitter woman, considering her contributions to the family a duty, not a labor of love, and resenting Liz. When Liz's school is to be evacuated to the country because of the bombings of London, Liz is overjoyed to be escaping this dismal existence.

Liz is to board with the Breretons, an upper-class family. For months, Liz feels the outsider. Eventually, however, she becomes a part of the family, sharing in their joys and their tragedies. And tragedies there are. The older son, Simon, leaves school to join the armed services. Eventually, he is declared missing in action; when the family finally learn that he has been taken prisoner by the Germans, they can only rejoice, for he is still alive. Likewise, the grandfather, a former admiral, and Ben, the middle son and Liz's favorite, join in a makeshift evacuation of Dunkirk after the battle. The grandfather is killed, Ben injured. Their part in the rescue mission vividly illustrates the chaos, the terror, and the cruelty of war.

At times, Liz finds the war exciting, and certainly all the Londoners must live life to its fullest. She does, however, see the heartbreak as well, and gains particular insight into the effect of war on women:

> "We got to wait, Liz. We always got to wait. Don't you think your ol Grand don't know—awaitin' all them months for him.... We got to eat and wash and cook and sew—and wait, with everythin' hurtin' inside us so we can 'ardly breathe. That's what war is to us women, Liz" (141).

His Enemy, His Friend by John R. Tunis is a powerful statement about the nature of war, of nationalism, of individual conscience, of principles. In June of 1944, in a coastal French village, Nogent-

Plage, Feldwebel Hans must face an agonizing decision. He has been a member of the occupation forces for years. Although he comes from an aristocratic family with a strong military background, he is an indifferent soldier. However, his superiors keep him there because he gets along so beautifully with the villagers. His love of music, his basic decency, his ability as a soccer player endear him to the French people. He, in turn, has become fond of all of them, teaching the young ones how to play soccer, helping the adults with difficult decisions, even befriending the animals in the village.

Because an invasion is expected, a general is visiting the village, a key defense area. When he is shot by a terrorist, Hans's superiors order him to execute six of the villagers, all innocent, as an example. Among the six are an elderly priest, a young boy, and Varin, the schoolmaster, Hans's best friend and the father of Jean-Paul, a soccer player and a protégé of Hans. When Hans refuses to carry out the order, a superior, ironically Hans's godfather, appears. In the mass confusion that results, the order *is* given, and the six are killed. Later, we find that a war tribunal finds Hans guilty of war crimes, and he is sentenced to ten years of hard labor and labeled "The Butcher of Nogent-Plage."

In 1964, Rouen, France, hosts an international soccer game between the French and the Germans. The star of the Germans is Hans, the star of the French, Jean-Paul Varin. In a game filled with action, tension and suspense, the Germans finally win. On their way home, they stop at Nogent-Plage. While the children are thrilled to see Hans, a superstar, older villagers, victims of the war, take him and the other Germans prisoner. When Jean-Paul arrives home, he tries to save his former enemy, his former friend, but a man kills Hans.

Although the coincidences are a bit hard to swallow, the book does seem believable, and it does a powerful job of showing the absurdity, the cruelty of war. When Hans and his grandfather discuss the upcoming execution, the older man sums up the necessities of war – one must be cruel to be a good soldier; one must obey orders above all for one's country. Hans, on the other hand, leans toward his conscience – "'What I am asked to do betrays myself. . . . He who witnesses a crime and does not protest, commits it himself'" (106–7). And the soccer game itself shows the absurdity and cruelty of nationalism, fans out of control, violence erupting in the stands, armed troops ready to act, all of this nastiness over a game that should stress athletics above all.

Both Jean-Paul and Hans realize separately that all nations are capable of the same cruelty and obsession that marked Hitler's Germany. At his trial, Hans says,

> "Someday you French and ... you Americans, even you Americans who are victorious and therefore think such a thing is impossible, someday you may also murder, torture, drop bombs, and kill innocent people in the name of some cause or in the belief that you are somehow defending your country while fighting in a foreign land, as we did" (124).

And Jean-Paul thinks:

> This sickness was the same malady which had swept the French stands in Rouen that afternoon.... "We cannot continue to cherish grudges. If we keep feeding this hatred handed down to us by our ancestors, our grandfathers and great grandfathers, where are we? Friends, what good are wars? Who ever won a war? Who ever profited from them in the end? ...Somehow, somewhere, we must break this evil chain and look on each other as human beings" (194–5).

Boris by Jaap ter Haar takes place in Leningrad, December 1942. Boris, probably around thirteen, has adjusted somewhat to the seige of the city by the Germans. Nevertheless, he is still haunted by nightmares because of the death of his father, who drowned while trying to bring supplies into the city, and he is terrified that his mother, ill and malnourished, will also die. The book does a marvelous job in showing the chaos, the tragedy, and the cruelty of war. Not only do we see the devastation, learn of the many lost lives of people Boris has known, and suffer along with the Russians when bombings occur, but we see the daily effects of poverty and illness. Indeed, the subject of food is paramount in the novel. At one point, on Christmas, all the children receive an invitation to attend a play. No one can concentrate, wondering if a meal will be served afterwards. We likewise learn the patience necessary to wait in long lines for a meager portion of watery soup. Natalie, an older friend, fakes her ration card, still carrying her brother and father, who have died earlier in the week. Such fraud, if detected, usually results in instant execution; nevertheless, need overcomes fear. It is Natalie who suggests to Boris that they travel into No-man's-land to find potatoes. It is this adventure that first opens Boris's eyes to the nature of war.

Captured by the Germans, the children naturally fear for their lives, but the Germans bravely cross the stretch of land, waving a white flag, to return the children to the city. "It was almost unbelievable, but they were going in the direction of the city. Again Boris looked at the face of the man who was carrying him. How was it possible that an enemy could have such a kind, friendly face?" (55). And when the Russians decide to shoot the Germans, fearing that they are not acting out of kindness, but may instead be spies, Boris throws himself in front of the German soldier.

> A desperate, helpless wave of passion swept over him; tears of rage against the hatred, terror and madness of war filled his eyes (65).

Finally, one Russian understands: "'Tell them they are free to go back. . . . Say to them that we are grateful; it would be shameful if we, in the brutality of war, should forget all humanity'" (65).

The next day, Natalie dies from weakness and starvation. And Boris has an equally dismal concern: Will his mother send him away to spare him? He cannot bear to leave her, for he knows that without him to get food, she will surely die.

In the midst of all this devastation, optimism still reigns. All realize that they must go on. Boris finds comfort in his mother's love and later in Natalie's diary, which captures her joy and her reverence for life. A soldier Boris encounters assures him that Leningrad will someday be rebuilt, "'. . . brick by brick, house by house'" (134). Suddenly, Boris is happy. He knows that he will never forget Natalie or his father; he realizes that

> . . .the battered city itself would never die; whatever was destroyed, whoever was killed, something would still remain— the spirit of the workers who died at their machines, the spirit

of the women who penetrated into No-man's land at the risk of
their lives to fell trees and drag back sledge-loads to the frozen
city. They didn't just bring warmth to the stoves—by their
courage, they lit fires in people's hearts (139–40).

The book ends as the Russians break through the German
lines. As Boris watches captured Germans being marched through
the streets, he feels only sorrow. Seeing one German whose eyes are
full of "pain and confusion and despair and grief" (148), Boris runs
into his path and puts a chocolate in his hand. An old woman
reacts: "'You did right.... What use is our freedom to us if we still
live in hate?' ...There was a pause, then most people nodded.
Because those who have suffered much, can forgive much..."
(149).

The story in *The Man in the Box: A Story from Viet Nam*
by Mary Lois Dunn is suspenseful, but often sentimental, often
trite. Chau Li is the son of a village chief, killed by the Viet Cong
after being tortured in the box, a tiny, cramped structure left in
the sun. Since that time, Chau Li has been the head of the household, taking care of his mother, his two younger sisters, his elderly
grandfather. When the Cong capture an American soldier and
imprison him in the box, Chau Li knows that he must save the
man. "'The spirit of my father sleeps in a secret place. If I do not
help that man, the spirit of my father will waken and come back
to haunt me'" (24).

Enlisting the help of Ky, an orphan and an opportunist, Chau
Li manages to remove the box and take it down the river to a cave
only he knows about. There he helps the soldier, David, pull
through. At one point, Chau Li must get food from a nearby
village. There he is befriended by a hateful old woman known in
the village as a witch. He also learns that American soldiers are
moving into the village. Thus he and David travel the difficult and
dangerous miles to reach the Americans. As the two of them are
about to be airlifted away, the pilot of the helicopter throws Chau
Li off. Soon the Viet Cong attack. The book ends with Chau Li
heading down the river toward Da Nang in search of his friend
David.

At first, the resourcefulness, the courage, and the honor of
Chau Li seem unbelievable. Then the reader realizes that living in

a war-torn country has forced the children to grow up far too early. Indeed, the entire novel points out the incredible cruelties and stupidities of war. While the author leans toward the American point of view, David admits that atrocities exist on both sides – and the author is brutally frank in discussing the horrors of war.

Likewise, Chau Li's devotion to David is easy to understand. Having saved his life, Chau Li of course becomes close to him. Further, he knows he can never return to his village – he has lost his entire family now – and we see his desperation for warmth and love from another human being.

One book does offer an alternative to war. Only two people die in *Enchantress from the Stars* by Sylvia Louise Engdahl, and neither one is developed fully enough for the reader to be moved at their demise. Rather, the book is about life – and the end of war. The book has several problems. Because of its many levels of interpretation – social criticism, history, anthropology, folklore – it is too complicated for most children; on the other hand, it is not sophisticated enough for adult readers. Likewise, the philosophy within is sometimes didactic and often tedious to a child, simplistic to an adult. Nevertheless, the book does raise important issues and gives an optimistic view of the future of mankind if we will only heed its message.

Elana, the protagonist, is an anthropological student in the distant future, living among totally, truly civilized peoples. She has sneaked aboard her father's starship, destined for Andrecia, a planet of Younglings, representative of the Middle Ages. Also on the planet are the Imperialists, a highly technological people paralleling modern man, there to colonize the planet. Eventually, Elana, her father, and her boyfriend Evrek coach Georyn, a Youngling, to fight the Imperialists. The action is reminiscent of folklore – the young son of a woodcutter, out to slay a dragon (the earth-moving machine), helped by the "enchantress" Elana with magic (her advanced knowledge and skills), and forced to endure many "tests" to prove his worthiness. We also see into the mind of Jarel, a physician of the Imperialists, who displays humaneness throughout and who questions the validity of colonization. Ultimately, we learn that both the Younglings and the Imperialists are going through evolution, that all civilizations will one day reach the stage of Elana's Federation, banishing the superstition of the

Younglings, advancing beyond the cold technology of the Imperialists, and relying on the amazing power of the human mind to perfect the world. The book shows that man does have the power to create harmony in the world.

VI. Conclusion

I might be driven to sell your love for peace,
Or trade the memory of this night for food.
It well may be. I do not think I would.

"Love Is Not All"
Edna St. Vincent Millay

The agents of death will not disappear. Nor will the suffering that people experience when they face the death of those they love, or their own death. What is the answer? Two haunting books sum up the central insight of children's literature on death.

John Donovan's central character, John Gridley, is indeed *Wild in the World*. He lives on Rattlesnake Mountain in New Hampshire, a savage place that most people avoid. He simply works, tending animals, hiring out at neighboring farms, keeping up his food supply by gardening, canning, and fishing. His only relief comes from the moonshine his older brothers have manufactured.

John is also surrounded by death. His mother died at his birth, his father and one brother committed suicide, his sisters — Winifred, Julie, and Faith — are dead, his brother Eben is dead, his brother Joseph was bitten by a rattlesnake, and Moses and Rachel, two other siblings, were burned in the fire that destroyed the old barn. Only Amos, Abraham, and John are left. Then Abraham dies from blood poisoning and Amos dies from a kick from a cow. Now John is totally alone.

> Evidently, John thought, everything that happens to you is out of your hands. You have a time to live; and childbirth, fire, your own shotgun, rattlesnakes, moving away to cities, fishhooks, cows, and diseases kill you. That is life, John thought (8).

160

Yet John feels guilt for some of these deaths. He feels so about his mother—"right at the beginning when he killed his mother getting born" (56)—and for Rachel and Moses. He had told them he was going to the barn, but instead went to the hen house. When the barn caught on fire, they rushed out to save him and were killed.

After John is left totally alone, a friend appears. At first, John thinks the animal is a wolf, but it turns out to be a dog. What follows is idyllic. The two become closer and closer, finally becoming inseparable. John names the dog Son, showing his incredible loneliness. At one point, he almost loses Son when a rattlesnake bites the dog. John is philosophical:

> Hell, all those brothers and sisters, and the mother and the father. Everyone dead. Just as natural as living. This dog is going to get swelled up until he bursts, John thought, and that will be the end of him (56).

Son lives, however—but John dies of pneumonia. Superstition makes the townspeople believe that the dog is actually a wolf, and they make plans to hunt it down, but nothing comes of their plans. After the people stop coming around, Son returns to sleep on John's bed, a reaffirmation of the close bond the two have shared.

Similarly, in *No More Tomorrow* by Reginald Ottley, the protagonists are an old man and his dog, Blue. The old man is a swagman—one who travels on foot through the outback of Australia looking for work (the "swag" is his blanket roll he straps across his shoulders). The dog is his ever-faithful companion, taught to obey only his master, to eat and drink only from his master's hand or at his master's orders.

Most of the people they encounter are decent, sharing their food, inwardly concerned about the old man who is obviously ill and obviously "mad" in his searchings for a vision somewhere over the horizon.

The writing is brilliant, capturing the wildness, the loneliness, and the dangers of the countryside. Yet sustaining the man and his dog are a love and companionship unmatched. As they wander, the old man recalls his past: the time he had to save his little sister

Jeanie, who had fallen down a well, and the deaths of his parents, his sister, and his beloved horse through fire when the man was only a boy of fifteen.

Eventually, during a dust storm, both are hit by a truck out of control. Here, the book covers the wanderings of the dog, who encounters angry cattle and vicious men hunting wild dogs. He must suffer incredible hunger, thirst, fatigue, and a bullet wound.

The two are reunited at the end, but the man and the dog are both soon to die. No matter. In this wonderful story of love and devotion, the reader sees the ultimate answer to death: living to the fullest, loving to the fullest.

Bibliography

For Adults

Allen, Woody. "Death Knocks." In *Literature, The Human Experience.* Ed. Richard Abcarian and Marvin Klotz. New York: St. Martin's, 1982. 1144-1151.

Arbuthnot, Mary Hill, and Zena Sutherland. *Children and Books.* 4th ed. Glenview, Illinois: Scott, Foresman, 1972.

Becker, Susan. "Helping Children Think About the Unthinkable." *Instructor,* September, 1983: 86-89.

Bettelheim, Bruno. *The Uses of Enchantment.* New York: Knopf, 1976.

Dickey, James. *Deliverance.* Boston: Houghton Mifflin, 1970.

Fulton, Robert. "On the Dying of Death." In *Explaining Death to Children.* Ed. Earl A. Grollman. Boston: Beacon, 1967. 31-50.

Grollman, Earl. *Explaining Death to Children.* Boston: Beacon, 1967.

Hemingway, Ernest. "The Short Happy Life of Francis Macomber." In *The Short Story: Form in Transition.* New York: Scribner's, 1969. 404-433.

Jacobs, Paul. "The Most Cheerful Graveyard in the World." In *The Borzoi College Reader.* 5th ed. New York: Knopf, 1984. 816-823.

Kastenbaum, Robert. "The Child's Understanding of Death: How Does It Develop?" In *Explaining Death to Children.* Ed. Earl A. Grollman. Boston: Beacon, 1967. 89-108.

Lindemann, Erich. "Symptomatology and Management of Acute Grief." *Journal of American Psychiatry,* September, 1944: 141-148.

Mackey, James A. "Living with the Bomb: Young People's Images of War and Peace." *Curriculum Review,* May, 1983: 126-9.

Mitford, Jessica. *The American Way of Death.* New York: Simon & Schuster, 1963.

Moller, Hella. "Death: Handling the Subject and Affected Students in the Schools." In *Explaining Death to Children.* Ed. Earl A. Grollman. Boston: Beacon Press, 1967. 145-170.

Ross, Eulalue Steinmetz. "Children's Books Relating to Death." In *Explaining Death to Children.* Ed. Earl A. Grollman. Boston: Beacon, 1967. 249-272.

For Children

Abbott, Sarah. *The Old Dog.* Illus. George Mooniak. New York: Coward, McCann and Geoghegan, 1972.

163

Aesop's Fables. Kingsport, Tennessee: Grosset & Dunlap, 1947.

Alexander, Sue. *Nadia the Willful.* Illus. Lloyd Bloom. New York: Pantheon, 1983.

Anderson, Leone. *It's Okay to Cry.* Illus. Richard Wahl. Elgin, Illinois: The Child's World, 1978.

Angell, Judie. *Ronnie and Rosey.* Scarsdale, New York: Bradbury Press, 1977.

Armstrong, William. *Sounder.* New York: Harrow, 1971.

Arundel, Honor. *The Blanket World.* Nashville, Tennessee: Thomas Nelson, 1973.

Bach, Alice. *Mollie Make-Believe.* New York: Harper & Row, 1974.

Bartoli, Jennifer. *Nonna.* Illus. Joan Drescher. New York: Harvey House, 1975.

Bauer, Marion Dane. *Shelter from the Wind.* New York: Seabury, 1976.

Beatty, Patricia. *A Long Way to Whiskey Creek.* New York: Morrow, 1971.

Beckman, Gunnel. *Admission to the Feast.* Trans. Joan Tate. New York: Dell, 1973.

Bosse, Malcolm J. *Ganesh.* New York: Crowell, 1981.

Brancato, Robin F. *Facing Up.* New York: Alfred A. Knopf, 1984.

Bridges, Sue Ellen. *Home Before Dark.* New York: Bantam, 1976.

Brooks, Jerome. *Uncle Mike's Boy.* New York: Harper & Row, 1973.

Brown, Margaret Wise. *The Dead Bird.* Illus. Remy Charlip. Eau Claire, Wisconsin: E.M. Hale, 1938.

Buck, Pearl. *The Big Wave.* Illus. Hiroshige and Hokusa. New York: John Day, 1947.

Bunting, Eve. *The Empty Window.* Illus. Judy Clifford. New York: Varne, 1980.

————. *The Happy Funeral.* Illus. Yo-Dinh Hai. New York: Harper & Row, 1982.

Burch, Robert. *Simon and the Game of Chance.* Illus. Fermin Rocker. New York: Viking, 1970.

Burton, Hester. *In Spite of All Terror.* Illus. Victor G. Ambrus. Cleveland, Ohio: World, 1969.

Buscaglia, Leo. *The Fall of Freddie the Leaf.* New York: Slack, 1982.

Byers, Betsy. *Good-Bye, Chicken Little.* New York: Harper & Row, 1979.

Cameron, Eleanor. *Beyond Silence.* New York: Dutton, 1980.

Carrick, Carol. *The Accident.* Illus. Donald Carrick. New York: Seabury, 1977.

————. *The Foundling.* Illus. Donald Carrick. New York: Seabury, 1977.

Carner, Chas. *Tawny.* Illus. Donald Carrick. New York: Macmillan, 1978.

Chambers, Aidan. *Dance On My Grave.* New York: Harper & Row, 1982.

Chandler, Linda. *Uncle Ike.* Illus. Paul Behrens. Nashville, Tennessee: Broadman, 1981.

Church, Alfred, ed. *The Iliad and the Odyssey.* New York: Macmillan, 1964.

Cleaver, Vera, and Bill Cleaver. *Grover.* New York: Signet, 1970.

————. *A Little Destiny.* New York: Lothrop, Lee and Shepard, 1979.

————. *The Mimosa Tree.* Philadelphia: Lippincott, 1970.

————. *Where the Lillies Bloom.* Illus. Jim Spanfeller. Philadelphia: Lippincott, 1969.

Cohen, Barbara. *Thank You, Jackie Robinson.* Illus. Richard Guffari. New York: Lothrop, Lee & Shepard, 1974.

Cohen, Miriam. *Jim's Dog Muffins.* Illus. Lillian Hoban. New York: Greenwillow, 1984.

Colman, Hilda. *Sometimes I Don't Love My Mother.* New York: Vagabond, 1977.

Collier, James Lincoln, and Christopher Collier. *My Brother Sam Is Dead.* New York: Four Winds, 1974.

Cooper, Susan. *Dawn of Fear.* New York: Harcourt Brace Jovanovich, 1970.

Coutant, Helen. *First Snow.* Illus. Yo-Dinh Hai. New York: Knopf, 1974.

D'Aulaire, Ingri, and Edgar Parid D'Aulaire. *Book of Greek Myths.* Garden City, New York: Doubleday, 1962.

_____. *Norse Gods and Goddesses.* Garden City, New York: Doubleday, 1967.

De Angeli, Marguerite. *Book of Nursery and Mother Goose Rhymes.* Garden City, New York: Doubleday, 1954.

De Bruyn, M.G. *The Beaver Who Wouldn't Die.* Chicago: Follett, 1975.

Dixon, Paige. *May I Cross Your Golden River?* New York: Atheneum, 1979.

Dobrin, Arnold. *Scat!* New York: Four Winds, 1972.

Dr. Seuss. *The Butter Battle Book.* New York: Random House, 1984.

Donnelly, Elfie. *So Long, Grandpa.* Trans. Anthea Bell. New York: Crown, 1981.

Donovan, John. *I'll Get There. It Better Be Worth the Trip.* New York: Dell, 1969.

_____. *Wild in the World.* New York: Harper & Row, 1971.

Dunn, Mary Lois. *The Man in the Box: A Story From Viet Nam.* New York: McGraw-Hill, 1968.

Emberley, Barbara. *Drummer Hoff.* Illus. Ed Emberley. Englewood Cliffs, New Jersey: Prentice-Hall, 1967.

Engdahl, Sylvia Louise. *Enchantress from the Stars.* Illus. Rodney Shackell. New York: Atheneum, 1971.

Fassler, Joan. *My Grandpa Died Today.* Illus. Stewart Kranz. New York: Behavioral, 1971.

Feagles, Anita Macrae. *The Year the Dreams Came Back.* New York: Atheneum, 1976.

Fitzhugh, Louise, and Sandra Scoppettone. *Bang, Bang, You're Dead.* Illus. Louise Fitzhugh. New York: Harper & Row, 1969.

Gardam, Jane. *The Summer After the Funeral.* New York: Macmillan, 1973.

Giff, Patricia Reilley. *The Gift of the Pirate Queen.* New York: Dell, 1982.

Greenberg, Jan. *A Season In-Between.* New York: Farrar, Straus & Giroux, 1979.

Greene, Constance C. *Beat the Turtle Drum.* Illus. Donna Diamond. New York: Viking, 1976.

Greenfield, Eloise. *Sister.* Illus. Moneta Barnett. New York: Crowell, 1969.

Gunther, John. *Death Be Not Proud: A Memoir.* New York: Harper & Row, 1949.

Gwynne, Fred. *The Story of Ick.* New York: Windmill, 1971.

Haar, Jaapter. *Boris.* Trans. Martha Mearns. Illus. Rien Poortvliet. New York: Dell, 1969.

Hammond, Janice M. *When My Dad Died: A Child's View of Death.* Ann Arbor, Michigan: Cranbook, 1981.

Hazen, Barbara Shook. *Why Did Grandpa Die?* Illus. Pat Schories. Racine, Wisconsin: Western, 1985.

Henry, O. *See* O. Henry.

Hermes, Patricia. *Nobody's Fault.* New York: Harcourt Brace Jovanovich, 1981.

_____. *You Shouldn't Have to Say Good-Bye*. New York: Harcourt Brace Jovanovich, 1982.

Hickman, Martha. *Last Week My Brother Anthony Died*. Illus. Randie Julien. Nashville, Tennessee: Abingdon, 1984.

Hoopes, Lyn Littlefield. *Nana*. Illus. Arich Zeldich. New York: Harper & Row, 1981.

Hosford, Dorothy. *By His Own Might: The Battles of Beowulf*. New York: Holt, 1947.

Hunt, Irene. *Up a Road Slowly*. New York: Tempo, 1974.

Hunter, Mollie. *A Sound of Chariots*. New York: Harper & Row, 1972.

Hurd, Edith Thatcher. *The Black Dog Who Went into the Woods*. Illus. Emily Arnold McCully. New York: Harper & Row, 1980.

Jacobi, Frederick, Jr., ed. *Tales of Grimm and Andersen*. New York: Modern Library, 1952.

Jacobs, Dee. *Laura's Gift*. Illus. Kris Karlsson. Portland, Oregon: Oriel, 1980.

Jewell, Nancy. *Time for Uncle Joe*. Illus. Joan Sandin. New York: Harper & Row, 1981.

Jukes, Mavis. *Blackberries in the Dark*. Illus. Thomas B. Allen. New York: Knopf, 1985.

Kantrowitz, Mildred. *When Violet Died*. Illus. Emily A. McCully. New York: Parents' Magazine Press, 1973.

Kaplan, Bess. *The Empty Chair*. New York: Harper & Row, 1975.

Kohn, Bernice. *One Sad Day*. Illus. Barbara Hohn Isaac. New York: Okpaku, 1971.

Lee, Virginia. *The Magic Moth*. Illus. Richard Cuffari. New York: Seabury, 1972.

L'Engle, Madeleine. *A Ring of Endless Light*. New York: Farrar, Straus & Giroux, 1980.

Line, David. *Soldier and Me*. New York: Harper & Row, 1965.

Little, Jean. *Home From Far*. Illus. Jerry Lazare. Boston: Little, Brown, 1965.

Logan, Jane. *The Very Nearest Room*. New York: Scribner's, 1973.

Lowry, Lois. *A Summer to Die*. Boston: Houghton Mifflin, 1977.

Lund, Doris. *Eric*. Philadelphia: Lippincott, 1974.

McKinstrey, Steve, and Lucy Rigg. *The Attic Treasure*. Seattle, Washington: Henry, 1982.

McLean, Susan. *Pennies for the Piper*. New York: Farrar, Straus & Giroux, 1981.

McLendon. *My Brother Joey Died*. Photographs by Harvey Kelman. New York: Julian Messner, 1982.

Madler, Trudy. *Why Did Grandma Die?* Illus. Gwen Connelly. Milwaukee: Raintree, 1980.

Malory, Sir Thomas. *The Boy's King Arthur*. Ed. Sydney Lanier. New York: Scribner's, 1952.

Mann, Peggy. *There Are Two Kinds of Terrible*. Garden City, New York: Doubleday, 1977.

Mazer, Harry. *When the Phone Rang*. New York: Scholastic, 1985.

Miles, Betty. *The Trouble with Thirteen*. New York: Knopf, 1979.

Mills, Claudia. *All the Living*. New York: Macmillan, 1983.

Miner, Jane. *This Day Is Mine*. Mankato, Minnesota: Crestwood House, 1982.

Ness, Evaline. *Sam, Bangs, and Moonshine*. New York: Holt, Rinehart and Winston, 1966.

Nye, Robert. *Beowulf: A New Telling*. New York: Hill and Wang, 1968.

O'Dell, Scott. *Island of the Blue Dolphins*. Boston: Houghton Mifflin, 1960.

O. Henry. *The Last Leaf*. Illus. Byron Glaser. Mankato, Minnesota: Crestwood House, 1980.

Oneal, Zibby. *A Formal Feeling*. New York: Viking, 1982.

Oppenheim, Joanne. *James Will Never Die*. Illus. Ture Kelly. New York: Dodd, Mead, 1982.

Orgel, Doris. *The Mulberry Music*. Illus. Dale Payson. New York: Harper & Row, 1971.

Ottley, Reginald. *No More Tomorrow*. New York: Harcourt Brace Jovanovich, 1971.

Paterson, Katherine. *Bridge to Terabithia*. Illus. Donna Diamond. New York: Avon, 1977.

Peck, Robert Newton. *A Day No Pigs Would Die*. New York: Dell, 1972.

Pfeffer, Susan Beth. *About David*. New York: Dell, 1980.

Pyle, Howard. *Some Merry Adventures of Robin Hood of Great Renown in Nottinghamshire*. New York: Scribner's, 1946.

Raskin, Ellen. *Figgs and Phantoms*. New York: Dutton, 1974.

Rhodin, Eric. *The Good Greenwood*. Philadelphia: Westminster, 1971.

Schotter, Roni. *A Matter of Time*. New York: Collins, 1979.

Sendak, Maurice. *Where the Wild Things Are*. New York: Harper & Row, 1963.

Seuss, Dr. *See* Dr. Seuss.

Shreve, Susan. *Family Secrets: Five Very Important Stories*. Illus. Richard Cuffari. New York: Knopf, 1979.

Slote, Alfred. *Hang Tough, Paul Mather*. Philadelphia: Lippincott, 1973.

Smith, Doris Buchanan. *A Taste of Blackberries*. Illus. Charles Robinson. New York: Crowell, 1973.

Stile, Norman. *I'll Miss You, Mister Hooper*. New York: Random House, 1984.

Stolz, Mary. *By the Highway Home*. New York: Harper & Row, 1971.

————. *The Edge of Next Year*. New York: Harper & Row, 1974.

Stone, Judith. *In the Jaws of Death*. Illus. Beth Hutchins. Milwaukee: Raintree, 1980.

Strete, Craig Kee. *When Grandfather Journeys into Winter*. Illus. Hal Frenck. New York: Greenwillow, 1979.

Stretton, Barbara. *You Never Lose*. New York: Knopf, 1982.

Stevens, Margaret. *When Grandpa Died*. Illus. Kenneth Ualand. Chicago: Children's, 1979.

Tobias, Tobi. *Petey*. Illus. Symeon Shimin. New York: Putnam's, 1978.

Tunis, John R. *His Enemy, His Friend*. New York: Morrow, 1967.

Viorst, Judith. *The Tenth Good Thing About Barney*. Illus. Eric Blagvad. New York: Atheneum, 1971.

Vogel, Ilse-Margret. *My Twin Sister Erika*. New York: Harper & Row, 1976.

Wallace-Brodeur, Ruth. *The Kenton Years*. New York: Atheneum, 1980.

Warburg, Sandol Stoddard. *Growing Time*. Illus. Leonard Weisgard. Boston: Houghton Mifflin, 1969.

Wersba, Barbara. *Run Softly, Go Fast*. New York: Atheneum, 1970.

White, E.B. *Charlotte's Web*. New York: Harper & Row, 1952.

Windsor, Patricia. *The Summer Before*. New York: Harper & Row, 1973.

Yolen, Jane. *The Stone Silenus*. New York: Philomel, 1984.

York, Carol Beach. *Remember Me When I Am Dead*. New York: Elsevier/Nelson, 1980.

Zemach, Margot. *Jake and Honeybunch Go to Heaven*. New York: Farrar, Straus & Giroux, 1982.

Zolotow, Charlotte. *My Grandson Lew*. Illus. Pene DuBois. New York: Harper & Row, 1974.

Index